FOREWOR

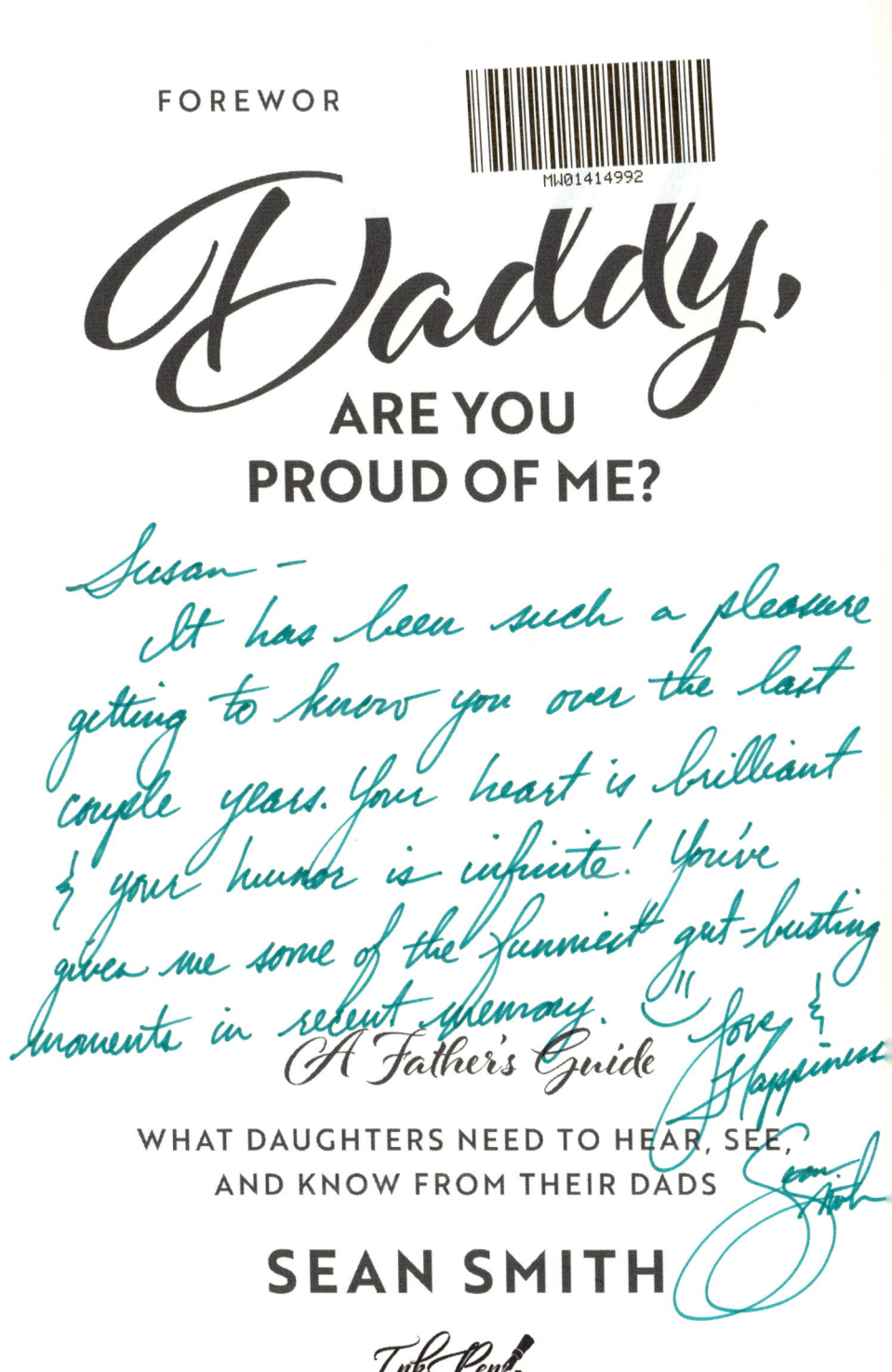

Daddy,
ARE YOU PROUD OF ME?

Susan —
It has been such a pleasure getting to know you over the last couple years. Your heart is brilliant & your humor is infinite! You've given me some of the funniest gut-busting moments in recent memory.
Love & Happiness
Sean Smith

A Father's Guide

WHAT DAUGHTERS NEED TO HEAR, SEE, AND KNOW FROM THEIR DADS

SEAN SMITH

Ink Pen
PRESS

MOORPARK, CALIFORNIA

Daddy, Are You Proud of Me? What Daughters Need to Hear, See, and Know from Their Dads
Published by Ink Pen Press
Moorpark, CA

Copyright © 2021 by Sean Smith. All rights reserved.

No part of this book may be reproduced in any form or by any mechanical means, including information storage and retrieval systems without permission in writing from the publisher/author, except by a reviewer who may quote passages in a review.

All images, logos, quotes, and trademarks included in this book are subject to use according to trademark and copyright laws of the United States of America.

ISBN: 978-1-7344076-0-0

Parenting / Fatherhood

Cover and Interior design by Victoria Wolf, wolfdesignandmarketing.com.

All rights reserved by Sean Smith and Ink Pen Press.
Printed in the United States of America.

QUANTITY PURCHASES Professional groups, clubs, and other organizations may qualify for special terms when ordering quantities of this title. For information, email info@CoachSeanSmith.com.

DEDICATION

This book is dedicated to my daughter, McKenna. You changed my life by making me a father and have given me more meaning than I thought was possible. You are the most amazing daughter imaginable, and you inspire me daily to be a better person. I am so very proud of you, sweetheart.

CONTENTS

FOREWORD BY
Jack Canfield vii

INTRODUCTION
A Message to Daughters 1
A Message to Dads 3
The Day I Became a Dad 9

CHAPTER 1
The Five Most Precious Words 15

CHAPTER 2
Separate Her Person from Her Performance 21

CHAPTER 3
Tell Her She's Beautiful Inside and Out 31

CHAPTER 4
Learn How to Braid Her Hair 37

CHAPTER 5
Embrace Her Changing Body 41

CHAPTER 6
Show Her What Respect Is 45

CHAPTER 7
Love and Respect Her Mom, No Matter What 49

CHAPTER 8
Don't Always Be a "Father Fix-It" 53

CHAPTER 9
Teach Her How to Use Tools 61

CHAPTER 10
Open Your Heart to Her 65

CHAPTER 11
Let Her See You Cry 73

CHAPTER 12
Master Your Emotions 83

CHAPTER 13
Clear Your Pain 105

CHAPTER 14
The Total Truth Letter 117

CHAPTER 15
Discipline with Love 123

CHAPTER 16
Celebrate Her Uniqueness 129

CHAPTER 17
Value Her Voice 135

CHAPTER 18
"Replacement Parents" 141

CHAPTER 19
Be Her Biggest Fan 151

CHAPTER 20
Don't Be a Disappointed Dad 155

CHAPTER 21
Become the Man You Want Her to Marry 159

CHAPTER 22
Protect Her Dreams With Everything You've Got 165

CHAPTER 23
She Will Always Need You 175

THANK YOU, DAD 179

TIPS FROM OUR COMMUNITY 181

ONLINE RESOURCES 197

ACKNOWLEDGMENTS 199

ABOUT THE AUTHOR 203

FOREWORD BY

Jack Canfield

THIS WONDERFUL BOOK WILL DO two major things for you as a father with a daughter. First, it will help you increase her confidence, self-esteem, and joy, no matter how old either of you are or what the current status of your relationship is. Second, it will help you increase the emotional control and happiness in your own life, providing a better connection to your daughter, yourself, and all other loved ones.

Self-esteem has been the core focus of my life's work, dating all the way back to my days as a public school teacher in inner-city Chicago. I learned very quickly back then, and have seen it confirmed for many decades in my work as a personal development leader, that high self-esteem and success go hand in hand.

In fact, my studies have proven they are inextricably intertwined in an upward, spiraling cycle. High self-esteem causes people to get into motion quicker, take more risks, and create more results. More results in turn increase self-esteem, which leads to taking more action and so on.

As Sean so clearly points out, the self-esteem cycle for women has a *direct connection to their fathers*.

Now, it's one thing to know about a concept such as self-esteem, but it's another to be able to present the discussion in such an extremely clear way so that it is easy to understand how to build self-esteem from a foundational, yet practical, perspective. Sean has done exactly that in this timeless book.

Rarely do books have such concrete and implementable teachings that you can literally act upon today. But after reading the very first draft of this book, which was less than a third of what you now have in your hands, I found many valuable points that I instantly put into practice with my own stepdaughter.

Because of Sean's depth of commitment, attention to detail, personal experience, and ability to communicate otherwise confusing principles as clearly as he does, you will not only get a clear understanding of the empowering principles in this book, you will know how to immediately infuse them into the relationship with your daughter.

As I write this I am remembering Sean in the early days of his journey when he was attending and then assisting in my weeklong seminars, putting everything he could into action. He would repeatedly absorb, implement, and immediately teach what he was learning to others. Eventually, I asked him to train on stage with me. I can personally attest to the hard work, dedication, and unwavering commitment he has to teaching these concepts because I've seen it over and over with my own eyes.

It is a major highlight of my life to see all of that time—literally thousands and thousands of hours—come together so beautifully into this wonderfully impactful book with such an empowering and transformational message.

I know you will enjoy reading it, as I did. But what I'm more excited about is the positive effect it will have on the self-esteem, happiness, and joy in your precious daughter(s).

With great love for you and your children.

—Jack Canfield, Coauthor of the *Chicken Soup for the Soul*® series and *The Success Principles*™, and *How to Get from Where You Are to Where You Want to Be;* Founder, *Self-Esteem Seminars.*

INTRODUCTION

A Message to Daughters

IF YOU ARE A WOMAN READING this book, I see you, and I'm proud of you. This book isn't written directly TO you, but you might find that it's definitely FOR you, especially if you see yourself in one or more of the five most common low self-esteem patterns for women in Chapter 1. And please, please, please write a total truth letter, found in Chapter 14, to your father. That one exercise has transformed, healed, and liberated more women than I can count.

Let this be a special invitation for you to eavesdrop on a conversation between your dad and me, as well as all the influential men in your life. Like many women before, you may find it to be deeply meaningful and impactful. That is my wish and intention as you journey through these pages.

On behalf of all men, we don't hurt or neglect with malice or evil intentions, I promise—especially the precious little girls we helped to create. We don't know how to do better by you. If we did, we would. But we're trying. Please know we're trying our best.

My wish for you, as a woman, is that these words land gently on your heart, where they are needed, to serve or heal you in some way. I didn't initially write this book for women and won't be speaking to you directly in these chapters, but this message has provided unexpected healing for many women who've read it, regardless of whether their father is still alive or even open to this conversation. No matter where you are and what your relationship is with your dad, it can get better. I promise you. Allow this book to open that door of healing for you.

And, if you find yourself getting emotionally triggered as you read, remember—I'm a life coach! There are numerous resources online, found in the back of this book, to support you with whatever comes up. Please don't try to navigate difficult emotions alone. That should never be a D.I.Y. project. We've got you.

A Message to Dads

THERE'S NOTHING LIKE BEING A DAD.

But fathering a daughter ain't easy! It's a very tall and sometimes extremely difficult task. I honor you for being the kind of man who cares enough to pick up a book like this and read it. We need more of you in this world, protecting and empowering our girls and women.

My relationships with my son and daughter, both teenagers as I finish this book, are incredibly important to me. What's so fascinating is how unique each of those relationships is. My son needs different things from me than my daughter does. He sees me differently, watching me through a different lens. Like all little boys, he wanted to be like his dad, as I was the default role model of what a man is and who he can become. I have a lot to share about the father/son relationship and parenting in general, but those topics will have to wait for different books. (more information on masculinity can be found in the Online Resources section in the back of this book)

This book is for dads with daughters. Just writing those words gives me a shiver. The father/daughter relationship is a very tender one. But I didn't learn the true depth of the responsibility we have as dads until I became a life coach for women!

Ninety-five percent of my clients have been female, something I never intended and couldn't understand until recently. Now that I'm older and a bit wiser, I know that it was a divine appointment for me to learn what I needed to learn about two things: 1) the fragile relationship between a father and his daughter and 2) healing my own relationship with my mom. (That's a deep one and also the subject of a different book. So deep, in fact, that I wrote and performed a one-man play about bullying my mother and my ultimate path to self-forgiveness that you can watch if you like. You'll find a link at the end of the book.)

As a life coach for women, I have learned so much about the female mind, feminine energy, and the woman's journey in a world dominated by the pursuit of power. I've attended and hosted over 350 days of live seminars and workshops, and created well over 2,000 hours of audio and video programs, all serving mostly women. On top of that, I've coached hundreds of women in my one-on-one programs and spoken on numerous stages before mostly female audiences.

I've done a lot of work in this arena. This book comes to you after thousands and thousands of hours studying and serving women in a personal development context, helping them to be more successful in their businesses and more balanced in their personal lives.

After all of that time, the biggest lesson I've learned is the very clear conclusion that the two main challenges women face, that affect nearly all areas of their lives, are self-esteem and confidence. But self-esteem (I'll be using self-worth and self-value interchangeably) is *by far* the bigger problem.

Consider a few staggering statistics on female self-esteem:

By age thirteen, 53 percent of American girls are "unhappy with their bodies." By age seventeen, that figure increases to 78 percent, nearly four out of every five girls. ("Body Image & Nutrition." *Teen Health and the Media*. University of Washington. 2017)

Seven in ten girls believe they are "not good enough" or "do not measure up" in some way, including their looks, school performance, and relationships. ("Real Girls, Real Pressure: A National Report of the State of Self-Esteem." The Dove Self-Esteem Fund. 2008)

Seventy-nine percent of girls with low body esteem say they opt out of important life activities, such as trying out for a team or club and engaging with family or loved ones. ("Dove Global Girls Beauty and Confidence Report." The Dove Self-Esteem Fund. 2017)

One in four girls fall into a clinical diagnosis of depression, eating disorders, cutting, or other mental/emotional disorders. (*The Triple Bind*. Steven Hinshaw. 2009)

These statistics are sobering, to say the least, and hopefully paint a clear picture that a lack of self-esteem has become an epidemic in girls and women. The Dove research found that low body image has a lasting impact on a girl's confidence, resiliency, and life satisfaction, causing them to be more likely to succumb to beauty and appearance pressures, often withdrawing from fundamental life-building activities. So girls' happiness is quite literally on the line here, as it is directly correlated to self-esteem, especially related to physical appearances.

While we often lump self-esteem and self-confidence together as the same thing, they are, in fact, different. Self-esteem is how we perceive our value as a person; self-confidence is how we perceive our ability as a performer. For nearly all women, low self-esteem is the main factor that causes their fears, sabotage, self-destructive behaviors, and lack of happiness or fulfillment in their lives.

Why does all of this matter to you as a dad? Because...

> You are the primary source of your daughter's self-esteem.

This is the second biggest and most surprising lesson I've learned coaching women. Their self-esteem is significantly molded by their relationships with their fathers. This is true most especially during the formative ages of six through twelve, where the foundation is set that they carry through the rest of their lives.

I learned this because the nature of my work is helping women heal their pasts by going into their conscious or subconscious memories to find the origin of their self-esteem problems. And 90 percent of the time, we would land squarely on their daddy issues. As it became an undeniable truth in my work, it started to change the way I understood and, therefore, fathered my own daughter.

That is precisely why you're reading this book.

What poses a huge problem is that dads don't know about this connection between fatherly pride and self-esteem, so we aren't adequately equipped to create the positive programming in our daughters that will lead to higher levels of self-worth and greater, sustained success and fulfillment in life. However, the answer is simple, the process possible, and the effects profound. I wrote this book to be the guidepost for men wanting the most for their little girls.

The daddy conversation brings some women to immediate tears, makes others angry, and causes some to smile big. As fathers, we play such important roles in their growth, but most of us were never told that. We didn't get the memo, and these little girls didn't come with manuals.

We're mostly flying blind here, trying to give what we think our daughters need but from a grown man's, and likely a wounded boy's, perspective. This is quite literally an impossible task unless we hear from the women.

Consider this book exactly that.

This is not a crusade to bash or blame men, or masculinity, in any way. We are doing the best we can. I just want to share what all these women have taught me so more men can learn what I've learned and more of our little girls, no matter their age, can be helped and healed. This is a new calling for me, to educate men about this beautiful relationship with their daughters and to bring forth an awareness that us guys generally don't have because we were never taught it growing up.

I have the gift of foresight because my coaching experiences with adult women taught me things I would have never known otherwise, and it changed the way I parented my daughter, McKenna. (You'll meet her in Chapter 10.) I kept hearing myself say, "*Someone should write a book teaching dads how to protect and restore their daughters' self-esteem.*" So, after several years, I decided to become "someone."

If you have a small daughter or no children yet, think of this as a voice from the future. Learn from the lessons I have discovered coaching women with emotional wounds so you can plant the right seeds that will eventually grow into social independence, emotional strength, and core happiness.

If you have a preteen or teenage daughter, you are right in the middle of the most formative years. I'm sure you're already buckled up, and now you'll have some new tools and concepts to put into play.

If you have an adult daughter, please don't feel as though it's ever too late to heal a heart, yours and hers. She is, and always will be, your little girl, wanting and needing her daddy's love and pride. Your relationship and her self-esteem can always be nurtured, mended, and strengthened.

Gentlemen: one final thing before we kick off—I suggest getting a picture of your daughter or daughters to use as your bookmark while you read. ;)

The Day I Became a Dad

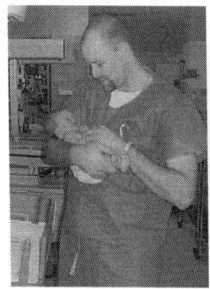

FEBRUARY 10, 2002.

"Is our baby going to be okay?"

That's the only question I have on my mind as we wait in the hospital room, looking at the monitors.

Every time my wife has a contraction, the baby's heart rate falls to a dangerous level. The doctor says the umbilical cord is wrapped around the baby's throat, making a normal delivery extremely risky.

So the decision is made, an easy one, really: C-section. The doctor tells us, *"You're going to have this baby at ten p.m."*

After all the uncertainty, it is very surreal to have an exact time scheduled for the birth of our child. And at this point, we still don't know if it's a boy or a girl—nor do we care. We just need this baby to live.

The minutes are passing fast and slowly at the same time. I feel a calm excitement. This is it. The time is here. I'm actually going to be a dad. Let's do it.

I am twenty-eight years old, and I know that what's about to happen next is going to change my life completely. I just don't know how much, how fast, or how deeply emotional it's going to be.

I put on my gown, hair net, and shoe covers as they prep Cybil for the operating room. She's as beautiful as I've ever seen her. In this moment, I have so much love and gratitude for my wife. Whatever she's about to go through in that room, I'm in.

Next thing I know, we're inside the operating room, Cybil on the table with a small curtain over her neck so she can't watch the operation. Given her history of passing out at the sight of blood, that's probably best.

I'm hovering above her head as the anesthesiologist monitors the concoction of medicines pumping through her body. I'm also peeking over the curtain to my right so I don't miss a single detail of the surgery.

I watch the incisions. I see the surgeon create a tiny hole in her stomach, way too small for a human to pass through. And then he reaches in and squeezes out this little head, all slippery and slimy and shiny.

That's my child.

I'm watching this baby enter the world mad as hell because of all this new, cold, and bright light. And I still don't know if this thing is a boy or a girl.

The doctor says he has to reach down and get a better grip under the shoulders to pull it out. So, for this very brief moment in time, a tiny human head is protruding out of my wife's belly, a scene straight out of the movie *Alien*.

And then, finally, they get the baby all the way out, still attached by the umbilical cord, and I hear the announcement. "*It's a girl!*"

A girl. A little girl. *My* little girl. Holy crap. After cutting the cord, they bring her over to the tiny bed under the heat lamp so she can get some warmth. I don't have any idea what I'm supposed to do, what the rules are. Truthfully, I'm in shock and proud of myself for remaining conscious and still standing upright.

"*Can I touch it?*"

When they give me permission, I place my hand on top of hers, she wraps her delicate fingers around my suddenly huge pinky and holds it tightly.

I just became a daddy.

I'm hers. Forever.

The intense curiosity of this moment is so powerful. All I can do is stare at all the little parts of this human that I've co-created. And for some unknown reason, I keep being drawn to her tummy. Watching the rhythm of her breath is intoxicating.

Seeing her images on ultrasound was cool, but looking at her in real life is breathtaking.

They put her into my arms, and I start to melt. (I'm crying now as I write, just thinking about that moment, reliving the preciousness and vulnerability I felt.)

As I look down at her little hand wrapped around my giant pinky, I promise myself this bond will never be broken. I know, in this moment, that I will fight any monster for her, protect her from any danger. I would die for her in a second. I will work as hard as I can to make her happy.

Everything in my world has now changed.

If you're already a father, I'm sure you remember your daughter's birth like it was yesterday, right? There's a sacredness in that moment, when two opposing energies, the masculine and the feminine, the tough and the tender, are linked forever.

Behold the strength of a man and the softness of this precious little girl he created. Welcome to fatherhood. Your life will never be the same again.

If you're anything like me, looking at your little innocent baby girl brings you to your knees and you question everything you think you know about yourself.

Will I be strong enough to protect her against all the evils of the world? Will I be able to provide everything she wants in life?

Am I going to be a good dad?

Am I—enough?

For most fathers I've spoken to, seeing their baby daughters for the first time takes them deeply into their souls, bringing up all their doubts and fears about who they are as a father, as a provider, as a protector, and as a man.

I'm so proud of this little girl we've created. I want her to always know that. I can't wait 'til she's old enough to understand it when I tell her.

But the scariest truth, the one that still takes my breath away to this very day, is that...

I just hope she's proud of me.

CHAPTER 1

The Five Most Precious Words

"I AM PROUD OF YOU."

Unconditional love is often touted as the greatest gift you can give another person and, while it is a great ideal to strive for, *unconditional pride* is the best gift a dad can give his daughter. Why? Because a father's pride is a self-esteem injection for a girl, straight into her heart. And lack of self-esteem is the greatest challenge most women will face in their lifetime. It starts being built up or broken down when she is just a little girl, and her daddy, her first hero, her protector is the *main* influence on how much of it she keeps as she develops into a woman.

The self-esteem problem basically boils down to a feeling of being "not good enough" inside, which causes most women to search outside of themselves for external validation and worthiness. That habitual cycle usually leads to a variety of emotional coping mechanisms and unhealthy behaviors.

This low self-esteem creates one or more of these five common and problematic behavior patterns for women.

Low Self-Esteem Pattern #1: Constant *Sacrificing*.

Some women don't even dare to *have* a dream and, therefore, struggle to find joy as they manage their to-do lists and take care of everyone but themselves. They've convinced their hearts that it's easier not to have desires than to have them and not be able to achieve them, so they constantly sacrifice their goals and dreams.

Low Self-Esteem Pattern #2: Constant *Sabotaging*.

Some women dare to go after their dreams but constantly sabotage themselves because, underneath the effort, they don't believe they *deserve* to succeed. They rarely take committed action toward their goals and, therefore, rarely achieve them because their fears are too overwhelming. They live in consistent internal conflict and usually create a start-stop-start-stop pattern of effort that is exhausting.

Low Self-Esteem Pattern #3: Constant *Settling*.

Some women achieve many of their goals, only to see them slip away because they don't feel worthy of *sustaining* success. They climb to the top of many of the mountains but fall down from most of them. As a result, they tend to focus their energy on the less fulfilling goals (the smaller mountains) because letting those achievements slip through their hands doesn't hurt nearly as bad as the more important ones.

Low Self-Esteem Pattern #4: Constant *Self-Smothering*.

Some women have the ability to achieve all their goals and dreams but choose to dim their own lights or hide their accomplishments because they believe their success and happiness will threaten friends, family members, or other women. They live in a state of mild to moderate *self-induced depression* that's not caused by sadness but rather from suppressing their abilities, emotions, and celebration of themselves.

Low Self-Esteem Pattern #5: Constant *Suffering*.

Some women actually become *addicted* to the pursuit of perfection, accomplishing all or most of their education, athletic, career, and personal goals, maintaining a high level of tangible success and flawless appearance. But they don't ever feel true satisfaction, peace, or joy because their accomplishments never fill the emotional void, no matter how much they achieve or how perfect they appear. This becomes frustrating, infuriating, or hopeless because they can't understand why they're winning in their minds but unhappy in their hearts.

All of these patterns are different manifestations of the same root problem—low self-esteem—usually stemming from the same root relationship—their father. You. Me. Us.

It's nearly impossible, even with the best of intentions and circumstances, for the feminine to be raised and influenced by the masculine, either in close proximity or complete absence, without at some point feeling confused, neglected, or scarred.

This is not an attack on you or any other dads because I know it's never intentional and usually it's not conscious. But the issue is real and deserves our awareness and attention so we can heal hearts (both ours and theirs), strengthen relationships, and foster a deeper foundation of love and connection.

The five unhealthy extremes outlined above, as well as every variation and combination in between, are a result of self-worth struggles that the majority of women face. I saw it over and over and over again, enough for me to see this connection so clearly that, with my coaching clients, I began to immediately focus on self-esteem below the surface instead of how to succeed above the surface. I learned that for women, success without esteem is emptiness.

But the great news is that we, as fathers, can help prevent that with a few simple words and genuine actions that all start with awareness and improve with practice.

While we men are not usually programmed to speak openly about our emotions, including telling our kids how proud we are of them outside of their performance, we can all certainly learn how to accept this responsibility, for our daughters' sake. It may seem easier and come more naturally to say, "*I love you,*" but there is something magical about the word "proud" for our girls. It tells your daughter that you don't just love her as your child, you *like* her as a person. Your daughter knowing you like her is so significant because without that feeling an emotional hole is created in her heart. When little girls don't believe their daddy is proud of them, they will usually seek that missing approval from other men, or masculine environments, in some form or another, trying to fill this hole. That's a potentially dangerous road for her to follow as she enters her future relationships—romantic, professional, and personal.

As her dad, you're the best person to fill her heart with love and devotion, with the pride and esteem she needs, until she can nurture her own later in life and ultimately understand that she does not need to source them from someone else, including you. If she doesn't get your pride but seeks it from other sources, she is more likely to be rebellious, become defiant, abuse drugs or alcohol, develop an eating disorder, become an unhealthy overachiever, be promiscuous, experience depression, or create some other type of negative coping mechanism to deal with the void.

But it's critical to understand that the void isn't always a result of explicit neglect or pain; it can just as easily manifest from a lack of expressed pride and appreciation. In other words, you can be a physically and emotionally present, non-abusive, active, loving, protective provider with a good relationship with your daughter, happily married to her mother and still unintentionally create a void, due to an innocent lack of awareness.

Sometimes all it takes is a single moment: rolling your eyes, shaking your head, raising your voice, not following through on a promise to be at her recital, asking her why she got a B+ in that one class, or taking the puzzle piece from her hand and putting it where it goes instead of letting her figure it out on her own. I've seen all of these and many more similar moments cause self-esteem problems that can last a lifetime.

And all of this generally happens without conscious awareness on her part either. Women rarely understand intellectually what they're actually seeking emotionally, especially when it's deep below the surface and connected to their dads. So it's extremely difficult and frustrating for them to ever deal with the root issue unless they get professional help from someone competent in this particular arena.

If your daughter ever seems to resist when you tell her you are proud of her, that's okay. Say it anyway. Be relentless with it. Never let up. No matter how she reacts, she needs to hear it. In fact, the more she resists it externally, the more she seeks it internally.

Whisper in her ear how proud you are of her as she sleeps, her unconscious mind will receive it without any resistance at all because our unconscious minds never shut off. It's a great way to get that pride deep inside her subconscious belief system.

Share with other people, especially when she can hear you, how proud you are of your little girl. Sometimes hearing you tell other people about your pride is more validating than hearing it directly for herself. She might think you *have to* tell her you love her and you're proud of her as her dad, but she knows you don't have to tell anyone else. So when you do, it's something she will pay attention to, I promise.

And tell her often how much you appreciate her making you such a lucky dad.

CHAPTER 2

Separate Her Person from Her Performance

TELL HER YOU ARE PROUD OF HER every day, as a person, without conditions—not just her as a performer when she does well. Regardless of the outcome, be proud of her *always* in all ways. She's never trying to mess up, so don't punish her by withholding your pride when the results are poor. She NEEDS to understand that distinction. You're proud of her, no matter what. No. Matter. What. That's one of the most powerful gifts you can ever give her.

Even when she makes poor choices, separate her as a person from her decisions. You can be proud of her as your daughter and still not like her choices. Those are not inherently linked together, but most of us men were taught that they are. As a result, we parent the way we were parented, and most girls, therefore, think what they do as performers and who they are as people are forever linked so that they only feel good about themselves when they are performing well. And they'll tend to chase tangible rewards and approval for the rest of their lives.

Because this can be difficult, let me offer a couple of examples. Let's say she's nine years old and spills a colorful drink on your expensive white rug. Instead of throwing all of your pent-up anger at her with your loud booming voice, do whatever you can to muster up a smile, even a laugh, because her self-esteem is at stake in this very moment. Ask her if she's okay to show that you care about her feelings. And then ask her to fetch a towel or go get one yourself.

This is a tender, vulnerable, and defining moment for her. She didn't want to damage the rug, and she *never* wants to disappoint you. The more love and acceptance you can pour into the moment, the better the experience and the lessons will be for her. When your daughter knows that your highest priority is protecting her instead of punishing her, she will always know that being with you and sharing her life with you is safe.

And if you really want to create an empowering memory that she'll never forget, stop what you're doing, sit down on the floor with her, and help clean up the spill while talking to her heart. But don't tell her in that moment what she should have done differently or what she should do in the future. That's talking to her head as you focus on fixing the problem.

Now is not the time to correct; now is the time to connect. Tell her how proud you are of her, tell her you're not disappointed in her, and then ask her what she wants to talk about. After the mess has been cleaned, things have been put away, and the connection moment is complete, then you can talk about the behavior.

We, as men, tend to want to fix any problem in front of us immediately. But her learning will actually be much better when the correction takes place after the connection. Make sure her self-esteem is protected; then talk about the behavior. Sometimes, though, that won't even be necessary because she'll come up with her own behavior lessons, which is the absolute best-case scenario. Give her that time and space to self-correct whenever possible.

Let's take something maybe a little more challenging. Let's say your teenage daughter gets suspended from school, comes home drunk, or does anything else that's a serious offense in your mind. Still, protect her heart before doling out the punishment.

These acts of defiance or deviance are generally calls for help, not calls to be punished by her dad. Of course, I'm not saying you shouldn't punish when her behavior warrants it, but understand that the behavior is likely a symptom of a deeper issue. She's usually looking for attention or affection or approval of some kind when she does things that are clearly out of bounds. These are not natural behaviors for young girls—there is generally a purpose behind them.

Be with her. Listen to her. See her. Do it all with love first, not anger. Be emotionally safe, letting her feel that you love and approve of her as a person, even though you don't like or approve of the behavior choices. I guarantee that will go such a long way in helping her change her behavior, much better than threats, yelling, or shame.

Ask her what she was trying to achieve or who she was trying to impress with her choices. Ask her if the behavior accomplished her desires (it rarely will). Then ask her if there's another way to accomplish those desires or whether the desires themselves are even worth trying to achieve. These are the kinds of exploratory questions that will help you get to the root of the behavior, help her better understand her own behavior, and increase the chances she will want to make changes on her own without even needing your admonishment.

This approach might not be easy to do at first because it's not our programmed response as men. It's probably not what your dad did with you when you spilled drinks and broke rules. He just didn't know. Forgive him, forgive yourself for any of the angry moments in the past, and be intentional in the future.

We tend to want to punish and correct because we don't like what just happened and we don't want it to happen again, which is understandable, of course. But if you understand human psychology, emotional punishment actually *increases* the chance that the negative behavior will be repeated because it's based on fear and threats without addressing the underlying causes of the behavior. And worse than that, it creates separation, anxiety and possibly resentment in your relationship with your daughter.

The physical damage to the rug or the rules that have been broken are already in the past and can no longer be prevented. But what's hanging in the balance is the emotional damage to your daughter's heart and her relationship to you when she makes mistakes or poor choices. Getting angry won't unspill the drink, nor will it unbreak the rules. But getting angry could scar her for life. I've seen it over and over and over again—even by good, loving dads who simply lost momentary control.

There is no feeling of approval or pride in anger, especially the way most of us men express our anger with our loud voices and threatening body language. It's scary and unsafe for girls to experience. I've coached many women who have visceral reactions of fear or even terror when men raise their voices at all, even if they're not angry or they are talking to someone else. Just the volume triggers the trauma. There can be a biological connection to the male voice being raised itself, regardless of intent. This is the possible damage we can unintentionally create when we yell in anger and they don't feel safe.

From a behavioral perspective, your daughter believing that you're angry at her as a person could cause her to be irrationally scared of making mistakes of any kind, large or small, for the fear of getting punished and disapproved of. In other words, her self-worth can become conditional upon her never making mistakes, always needing to be "perfect." That's not healthy and will not serve her happiness later in life.

The spilled drink incident is not a hypothetical example; it's from an actual coaching conversation of mine, although it was with a single mother, not a father, who was acting in a masculine role at the time. She was so angry because her daughter had unintentionally ruined her precious rug that cost her $2,000. So, I asked how much her daughter's self-esteem is worth that she *intentionally* ruined.

She, of course, said she didn't intentionally ruin her daughter's self-esteem, to which I replied, "*But you intentionally chose to yell at her. Same thing.*" That thought stopped her in her tracks, and she started crying because she didn't realize the damage that her anger had caused. There's no doubt that she herself had been yelled at as a child during a similar incident and was simply reacting out of her memory once her role changed to a parent. Her daughter's self-esteem was, indeed, worth infinitely more than that rug, and to my knowledge, she never yelled in a similar situation again.

There's a popular saying you've probably heard, "*Don't cry over spilt milk.*" My parenting add-on would be, "*Don't yell over spilt milk either.*" It does way too much emotional damage with little to no behavioral correction anyway. It's truly a Lose-Lose situation.

No matter what age your daughter is, remember the acronym **L.O.V.E.** to help you navigate these kinds of scenarios.

1) **Laugh**. Anger is dark; humor is light. Anything you can do to disrupt your anger trigger is positive for both you and her. Even if it's a small, barely audible giggle or a silent one inside your head, I promise you will respond more lovingly when you start with a chuckle.

2) **OKAY**. Ask if *she* is OKAY—her as a person, physically and emotionally. Even if the situation makes it seem weird to ask if she is okay, that's actually better. The immediate message is, "*Daddy cares about YOU first, things second.*"

3) **Volunteer**. Offer to help. If it's nonphysical, offer to talk. Don't jump in and immediately clean up her messes for her; that's

disempowering. Just be available to clean up her messes with her, physically or emotionally. And if she refuses, support her choice by letting her do it on her own.

4) **Embrace**. This has a double meaning. First, accept the situation and be as fully present in the moment as possible. Wishing it were different isn't going to change anything. Second, give her a big, huge hug that only a daddy can give. Completing a potentially negative incident with a loving hug is the perfect remedy for her heart—especially when it's accompanied with those magic words—"*I am proud of you.*"

Just like the concept I shared earlier about admonishment, when you tell her you are proud, don't make it about her accomplishments either. Make it just about *her*. In other words, be proud of her for who she IS, not only what she DOES. Another way to think of it is to appreciate her as a *person*, not as a *performer*. We are human *beings*, not human *doings*, so focus on her being more than her doing.

Give your girl the gift of feeling secure with herself, just because of her value as a person instead of her value being conditional upon what she does, such as her grades in school, her performance on the soccer field, or even how clean her room is at home.

We should never teach our daughters that their self-worth is conditional upon anything. Unconditional self-esteem leads to emotional balance, happiness, and confidence. Conditional self-esteem leads to emotional instability, addictions to external substances or judgments, and a never-ending search for validation.

One of the most dangerous emotional connections your daughter can make is between what she does as a performer and how valuable she is as a person. If she believes that her self-worth is only determined by her achievements, she will constantly be trying to make herself feel good through her accomplishments.

That connection usually causes emotionally extreme perfectionism, procrastination, compulsive overachievement, fears, and severely negative self-talk. If her self-esteem is at stake every time she has an opportunity to perform, then failure becomes emotionally devastating and quite scary. She will simultaneously be terrified of and addicted to performing. This is the root cause of so many women's performance anxieties and many other negative behavior patterns.

The reason this is so dangerous is that she will never find true self-worth through those tangible accomplishments. Adult women will often become workaholics or take jobs doing work they don't enjoy in an attempt to fill the void within. It leads to a constant pattern of trying to impress other people with their actions, always seeking approval.

For so many of the women I've coached, that has become a vicious behavior pattern. It is a never-ending game with no positive outcome. No matter how much she achieves externally, it won't ever be enough because *she* is not enough. When she believes that what she *does* isn't good enough, she will believe that who she *is* isn't good enough either if the two are connected in her mind.

As she grows, this may manifest into a fear of taking risks in general. She won't want to try for success if there's a possibility for her to be emotionally crushed when she fails. Again, this fear lives below the surface and isn't consciously created, so she won't be aware of what she's really searching for, making it almost impossible to fix the problem on her own without professional help or intervention. Let's do our best to make sure this person-performer attachment is broken.

This issue is a particularly difficult one for dads because, as men, we are overtly programmed to believe our value is tied to our performance. We develop much of our identity through competition as we grow up—especially in sports, whether it's an official organized league or on the playground amongst friends.

Boys always want to be the kid who can run the fastest, throw the best spirals, hit the farthest home runs, lift the heaviest weights, dominate on the basketball court, skate the fastest on the ice, etc. All of that is fine inside the ring of competitive sports, but it is a difficult habit to live with when it spills over into other areas of life and relationships, especially for our girls.

If the pattern isn't broken, your daughter will constantly compare herself to others, which is a *huge* problem for women anyway. In the teenage years, it often leads to emotional turmoil as our society and social media teach her to compete with the most popular girls at her school and celebrities on TV, always trying to outdo them.

She already has so many hormonal storms to deal with as she grows; this isn't a battle that serves her well, especially in today's social media world, where comparisons are amplified exponentially and destroy self-esteem faster than anything we've ever seen before. What she needs to know from you is that she is enough, exactly as she is, regardless of how she stacks up against others. Admittedly, this isn't always easy, but her heart and self-esteem are worth the effort.

Men have been programmed in such a macho way through our own experiences and in the media that *we* are the ones with the unhealthy connection between achievement and self-esteem. As boys, most of us were only taught what I call "performance pride"—where our fathers, father figures, athletic coaches, and other leaders only told us they were proud of us when we performed well. The opposite message, therefore, is that when we're not performing, we have little to no value or usefulness. So this will be healing for you, too, as you break that pattern with your daughter.

CHAPTER 3

Tell Her She's Beautiful Inside and Out

SOCIETY TEACHES GIRLS TO YEARN for being pretty on the outside. But that's emotionally dangerous because "pretty" is an external judgment. Girls are trained to seek other people's approval of them through their appearance—more makeup, less makeup, better makeup, more hair, less hair, better hair, different colored hair, less fat, more fat, smaller hips, bigger hips, smaller boobs, bigger boobs, rounder boobs, better butts, smaller lips, bigger lips, smaller noses, straighter noses, higher cheekbones, and better clothes—it's exhausting just writing those things, let alone living them!

The pressure around external appearance is much different for girls than it is for boys. Sure, us boys are usually taught to be some version of "tall, dark, and handsome" in order to be wanted, which causes many of us to try to get stronger, leaner, and keep all of the hair on our heads. (Or is that just me?) But our physical appearance is not so closely tied to our value like it is with girls and women. So we, as men, starting with our daughters, need to change that.

There's nothing wrong with women wanting to look pretty and absolutely nothing wrong with us as men using that word, as long as their self-esteem isn't at stake if other people don't like or approve of their external looks. That's the key distinction, wanting versus needing, similar to the achievement discussion from Chapter 2.

I like to think of it this way—*pretty* is the icing on the cake, but *beauty* is the cake. Pretty is based on external perception, on some set of standards determined by others, which can change constantly. What is considered pretty in a beauty pageant might be different than a cheerleading competition or a magazine cover or a photoshoot, or a wedding, or at school, or in a different country, or simply between two different people in the exact same setting.

But beauty is internal, based on value, not perception. Beauty is foundational, not superficial. Beauty is soul deep, not skin shallow. Beauty is constant, not temporary. Beauty is about presence, not image. Beauty is about who she is on the inside, not how her looks are perceived from the outside. And the most important piece is that beauty is controllable by the individual girl or woman, whereas the perception of "pretty" is based on other people's unstable and ever changing standards.

Because of all those distinctions, being beautiful is more important to girls' self-esteem than being pretty. Tell her often how beautiful she is in your eyes. Talk to her about the difference between the two, and then tell her how pretty you think she is as well. Putting them together is perfect as long as they are in the correct order and will help her deal with society's programming as she gets older.

If she's still young, your daughter may want to play dress up or pretend to be a princess. My advice is this: play along. Then when she's done playing, remember to tell her how beautiful and pretty she is without the dress. It's not about the dress or the hair or the makeup. It's about the sparkle that shines when she smiles, the love that lifts others when she laughs, the good feelings you get when she gives you a hug, and the pride you feel when you watch her play. Help her know how many other ways she is beautiful to you, not just pretty in her appearance.

Unfortunately, as your daughter continues to grow, society steps in and subjects her to supermodels and movie stars and other idols, matching these standards of genetic prettiness, who are often photoshopped beyond belief. (Think about that for a moment: Even the *models* aren't as attractive as the models!) Girls and women are subjected to so much judgment based on their looks that it becomes easy to compare themselves to the abundance of "celebrities" online, in magazines, and on TV that they wind up feeling "less-than" in so many ways.

Don't put glamorous or celebrity women down in your daughter's presence, but teach her the truth about their often altered reality and focus on lifting her up. We really have to remind our daughters how beautiful and pretty they are in today's world of social media comparisons. If they don't hear it from us first, they will likely turn to other men to find approval. You don't want her seeking self-esteem by chasing boys' approval and trying to make herself physically attractive with clothes or makeup, where she will be in a state of constant attention-seeking from people who are often emotionally unstable themselves! That's a potential cycle of misery.

If you continue to express your love for her and how beautiful she is, she will not succumb so easily to the images around her. When you constantly define "beauty" and "pretty" for her, she won't need the media to do it. Plus, if you don't ogle over supermodels in the latest *Sports Illustrated Swimsuit Edition*, or any supermodels for that matter, those images will influence her less too. Many women learned what men are attracted to and, therefore, what they should do to be attractive, by watching their father's reactions to women. Always remember, she's watching and learning from you.

To be super clear, there's absolutely nothing wrong with girls and women wanting to dress nicely and appear attractive because they enjoy it, but when they are searching for the attention or approval of others to fill their void of self-worth, it creates emotional turbulence. Your daughter may find herself feeling good with the attention she receives but feeling empty when the attention is gone, shameful about what she did to get it, or resentful because she feels like she always has to repeat the pattern to feel better about herself. It's exhausting.

If you, as her dad, give her attention and tell her she's beautiful when she's being her authentic self, it makes her feel good and encourages her to continue feeling comfortable being who she is because that's what she will connect to your praise.

Sure, as she grows she may experiment with different ways of wearing her hair and how to wear makeup and styles of dress, but she won't lose sight of who she is if you don't. If something she does brings out her beauty even more, tell her. But always reinforce that it's not the hair, makeup, or outfits that make her stunning and marvelous, rather it's her being true to herself.

Likewise, if she tries something and it diminishes her inner radiance, then let her know what you see. For instance, you can say, *"Sweetheart, can I share something with you about what I noticed when you wore that dress last night? To me, it seemed like you weren't as comfortable as you normally are. Would you agree?"* Asking for permission and agreement always makes the statement land easier and gives her the option to disagree.

You teaching her the difference between internal and external attractiveness and making it a constant conversation will do so much good for her emotional health and future relationships, I promise.

CHAPTER 4

Learn How to Braid Her Hair

GIRLS HAVE A VERY DIFFERENT RELATIONSHIP with their hair than boys do. Embrace that, and use it as a way to get closer to your daughter. Taking an interest in what's important to her, even if it's not important to you, lets her know that *she* is important to you. Don't try to force yourself to be happy with the act of braiding hair; find the joy in spending time with your girl.

If she's not into braiding hair, find out what she *is* into and do that. Play dolls with her, attend her tea parties, do a dance party, or take her on a date. Let her braid your hair or put makeup on you if she wants, even if it's just one time. Those memories are precious and priceless for her.

If your daughter is now older than the doll-playing and tea-party age and you didn't have these moments with her, you can still ask her if it's something she wants to do. Often, these desires are arrested in time for women, but they still exist. I've seen tremendous healing take place when adult women from twenty years old to seventy years old live out some of their little girl dreams with their dads, either in person or in their imagination. She may say no, but it's worth the shot to ask.

As fathers, we often find it easier to connect through pastimes we always enjoyed, like playing catch, building things, and horsing around, but it's important not to always take the lead in what activities you do. Let her choose, and you play along. That also teaches her that her choices are important to you because they're important to her.

You might not enjoy fake tea and cookies with stuffed animals or dolls, but you can enjoy your daughter's company. Find joy through her eyes and smiles instead of through the activity. Watch her light up, and let it light you up. It's about spending time on her terms and taking an interest in what interests her.

Ask her questions, and have her teach you how to do things she likes to do (like how to braid hair). When kids have a chance to share their knowledge and expertise, it helps them to grow in that skill even more. It also, and perhaps more importantly, gives them a wonderful sense of accomplishment and competence. Just as you might love to teach her how to hit a curveball, or swing a golf club, or dissect the characters of a play, she will love having the opportunity to teach you something you don't know.

If you want to spend time with her and you ask her to teach you something but she doesn't know what to teach you, simply give her your cell phone—almost assuredly she'll teach you something you didn't know about technology or social media. Our kids are growing up in a time so different from ours, and they seem to learn things, especially technology, much faster than we do. Tap into that energy, and experience the excitement they feel by mastering something new.

Don't allow yourself to get upset with the culture or technologies of her generation. It is much different than when you grew up, of course, as it is with all generations. But instead of using that as something to criticize or shame her with, embrace it and have her teach you about all the things you don't understand, or maybe don't even like. The role reversal of her teaching *you* is powerful.

It's also important to share what interests you so she gets to know you and what's important to you. Teach her what things were like before her time so she can appreciate all that she has now. There will be times when your daughter wants to do something for you, such as making or buying a present or throwing a party, and these conversations may give her the perfect idea. If she doesn't know you, she won't know what to do for you. In addition, sharing what interests you teaches her that her relationships won't always revolve around just her, which will benefit her in the future.

Tell her stories from before she was born, especially from your childhood. The more vulnerable or embarrassing, the better! Let her hear about and see your softer side, your younger side, your silly side. She only knows you as a grown man. When you allow her to see and imagine you as a little child, you're giving her a full perception of the boy inside the man, which is extremely important for women to understand, not just for their dads but for men in general.

You're nurturing a relationship and, in any relationship, the time you can spend together in joy is absolutely precious, so relish it, cherish it, protect it, and create happy memories as much as you can. When you show an interest in her interests, it sends the message that you love her and that you like spending time with her, and it will build your relationship because you'll always have something to talk about.

And remember, it's very important to continue these same conversations and connections as your daughter gets older as well, as best you can. Even if she declines the invites due to other circumstances, the fact that you asked is still comforting because it means you care and desire her company.

CHAPTER 5

Embrace Her Changing Body

I REMEMBER WHEN MY WIFE told me she was taking my daughter shopping for her first bra. I wasn't ready for that moment and my knee-jerk reaction was to avoid the discomfort with humor. But before I could get anything out of my mouth, my wife recognized my wheels spinning, raised her eyebrows, and leaned into me. "*She needs one. Don't make a big deal about it.*"

I am so thankful she stopped me in my tracks because I would have said something silly to pacify my own discomfort and, chances are, it would have landed awkwardly for my daughter. There's already a hormonal storm when girls' bodies start to grow and develop into womens'. The last thing we want to do is add to the storm with our own discomfort that could turn into body shame for her, which is a huge problem for many women.

Your daughter will always be your little girl, but her body is, of course, going to change. As she grows, continue to hug her, continue to cuddle and have tickle time, and do your best to stay comfortable with her changing body. And the same goes for the physical changes her body makes throughout her life, whether it's pregnancy, putting on weight, different hairstyles, facial features changing with age, etc. Make sure your love, pride, and affection toward her are not dependent on her physical appearance in any way.

Often dads shy away from their daughters physically, such as fewer hugs or tickling, especially when their bodies start to change. When you do that, it sends the message that you're not comfortable and, in turn, it makes her uncomfortable with her own body. If you show her that you're afraid of her changing body, even without meaning to, she will learn that something is wrong with it. That can lead to or strengthen a negative body image, which is something many, if not most, women struggle with because of how much focus society puts on women's physical bodies as a symbol of their value.

Even if you're not usually an emotionally expressive parent, start by giving her several hugs every day. Physical touch is incredibly powerful for all of us but especially for women. Nothing can replace a hug from dad. Author and therapist Virginia Satir proposed that we need four hugs a day for survival, eight hugs a day for maintenance, and twelve hugs a day for emotional growth. However you can, find a way to squeeze some hugs in each day for both of you.

For healthy self-esteem, we have to teach our little girls the following four healthy beliefs about their physical bodies.

1. *I am not my body.*
2. *My body was created perfectly.*
3. *My worth is determined by my being, not my body.*
4. *As my body changes, my self-worth stays the same.*

Guided by these beliefs, women are much more likely to love their bodies and maintain a healthy self-image through physical changes, including and especially the massive shifts that occur during pregnancy and after childbirth.

You can also teach your daughter about positive self-image by taking care of yourself and treating yourself with respect. If you walk around complaining that you're fat or ugly and she sees you as her handsome dad, it can confuse her, and she may even take those characteristics on and treat herself the same way. If there's anyone who can teach us unconditional love and acceptance, it's children. They do not have negative relationships with their bodies until adults, often their parents, teach them how to be mean to themselves.

The same is true for her mom, so make sure to share this concept with her (delicately, of course). It may be even more important for your daughter to see a woman treating her body well with healthy food, exercise, self-care, and loving words since she relates more closely to that female body than she does to yours.

Unfortunately, many women suffer from self-esteem issues tied to their physical appearance, and a lot of them aren't the best role models for our daughters. When you notice negative body image being displayed or portrayed in movies, or in the media, or in discussions among friends and family, use those examples to open positive conversations with your daughter about her body.

If she has already fallen into the negative body image trap, it's even more reason for you to help her understand how to handle negative head talk and turn it positive instead. Your voice matters to her, no matter how old she is.

CHAPTER 6

Show Her What Respect Is

THERE ARE NUMEROUS WAYS TO SHOW your daughter you respect her, but let's first talk about respect in general. Her thoughts and feelings about respect start when she's small, when she is being greatly influenced by her parents.

So, we will start with you, her proud pop. What does "respect" mean to you? I invite you to pause for a moment and define that word for yourself. It's a concept that controls many of our choices as men but rarely is it clearly defined or universally agreed upon.

Respect is defined in the dictionary as, "Esteem for or a sense of the worth or excellence of a person." I have no doubt if you're still reading this book that you have a profound respect for your daughter. The question is, does she *know* you respect her? If we were to ask her, would she say you do? Does she *feel* your respect? And how do you show her that respect?

There are a lot of theories on showing respect and what will make someone feel respected, but a good rule of thumb is the Golden Rule—treat others as you would like to be treated. If you're like me, you want to be treated with kindness, courtesy, sincerity, gratitude, and value. Therefore, I strive to live in such a way that others will experience these things when they interact with me.

An even better rule, in my opinion, is the Platinum Rule, which says treat others as *they* want to be treated. This requires you to know what other people want and how they want to be treated, which means you have to ask them. I suggest you ask your daughter what "respect" means to her and how she would like to be treated by people in general and, by you, specifically.

Of course, if your daughter is very young, she likely doesn't even understand the concept of respect, so you'll be teaching her what it means. Use your own rules about respect and live by them. Treat her with kindness, courtesy, sincerity, gratitude, and value, along with whatever characteristics imbue respect for you. In turn, she will connect your actions with her feelings and her experiences, and her definition of respect will likely be the same as or similar to yours.

As she grows older, continue to have open dialogues about respect because it changes as we move through different chapters of life. Ask her to define it. Ask her how it looks when she feels respected and how it looks when she doesn't. Ask her what she does in those situations when she feels disrespected and offer her alternatives if necessary. When appropriate, ask her what respect would look like in her intimate relationships, from both people's points of view.

Ultimately, respect is an internal game—what's most important is that she respects herself. Teach her that whatever she's looking for from others, including kindness, approval, attention, and love, she must give to herself first. A woman who respects herself naturally demands respect from others and won't tolerate poor relationships with people who don't show her respect.

You should also ask her what respect means to her friends, her teachers, her coaches, and her idols—and especially what respect means to and from boys since it's a concept that varies greatly between the genders. Don't immediately make her definition wrong if it differs from yours, just continue to discuss it in a healthy and productive way.

Always keep in mind that she's watching how respectfully you treat others, especially her mom. Let's go a little deeper into that conversation in the next chapter...

CHAPTER 7

Love and Respect Her Mom, No Matter What

HEAR ME OUT ON THIS ONE.

This might be tough to swallow for some men at first, depending on the relationship you have. But whether you like it or not, your daughter watches how you treat her mom and takes cues from you on what her life and her relationships will look like in the future.

> How you treat her mom determines how your daughter believes she deserves to be treated.

Please read that sentence over and over until it really lands for you because the gravity of it cannot be overstated. For that reason, love and respect her mom. No matter what. If nothing else, for your daughter's future.

Even if you don't agree with the things her mother does or the choices she makes or you don't like the person she is, it is imperative for your daughter's sake to treat her mom with kindness, courtesy, sincerity, gratitude, and value. Please trust me about how important this is. I've talked to hundreds and hundreds of women about it.

If it's difficult because of the conflict in your relationship with her mother, just imagine your daughter at the age of six years old watching, reading, and listening to every interaction. Or you might imagine that the words coming out of your mouth are being said by another man directly to your daughter. If you wouldn't want her ears to hear them, don't allow your mouth to say them.

This doesn't mean you don't communicate through your conflicts, but do it respectfully from your daughter's perspective, especially when she is present during that communication. In other words, would your daughter believe you are being respectful to her mom during conflicts? If the answer is no, don't say it. You being "right" and her mother being "wrong" in the argument isn't worth the effect it can have on your daughter, an effect that will likely last a lifetime and influence many areas of her success and happiness.

Her mom gave you the greatest gift when she nurtured and birthed your baby, and for that, you can always be grateful. Kindness and courtesy are common ways to treat all people, so I hope you can find it in your heart to always show these to her mom, even if she doesn't "deserve them" or show them back to you. Take the high road because your daughter's watching and learning.

If you're still together with her mom in a loving and nurturing relationship, this should be no problem. In fact, it's probably already in place or you wouldn't be in such a relationship. So keep it up.

However, if you're in a more difficult relationship, you may find it harder to respect her mom, let alone love her, amidst the conflict. I'm not asking you to love her as you may have at some point in the past but to choose love over destructive feelings, especially anger.

I know there may be times in any relationship that you will get angry, but it's important not to stay there. Process through your emotions until you get to the place of love. This can be done by acknowledging the feelings beneath it. We will dive much deeper into emotional management and control in Chapter 11. For now, just realize that when you do choose love and respect, you will find that it causes people you interact with to respond differently as well.

I say all of this because it's important for you to love and respect her mom so your daughter can see what she deserves in good, wholesome, loving relationships as well as broken ones. I know you want your daughter to always feel loved, so do your best to always act from love in all your relationships.

I also believe you want your daughter to be respected by other men, so in the toughest of times, ask yourself this question: "*How would I want my daughter to be treated right now?*" And then do that. I guarantee it will cause you to pause and choose your actions more carefully.

CHAPTER 8

Don't Always Be a "Father Fix-It"

IF YOU'RE LIKE MOST DADS, you likely feel the need or desire to protect your daughter at all times. I know I do. Even though your little girl came into the world tiny and helpless, she will continue to grow stronger and more independent every day, especially when you don't show up to fix all her problems. Protecting her from every potential danger or pain in the world actually stunts her emotional growth and self-esteem. Instead of trying to keep her safe from all harm, teach her how to build and use her own strength to keep herself safe as she grows older.

Think of the caterpillar transforming into the butterfly. If we were to cut open the chrysalis too early because we were uncomfortable with how much she is struggling inside, the result would be a caterpillar whose wings are too weak and underdeveloped to fly. Children build resiliency and learn lessons about themselves and their capabilities uniquely in times of struggle. For the most part, unless she's in danger of some kind, it's better to let her learn than it is to save her from failing.

Of course, we want to be our daughter's superhero, available and capable to rescue her from every situation. I know I did and often still do. But think about it—what kind of people need to be rescued? People incapable of taking care of themselves—victims. So each time we come in to save the day, we are telling her that she can't do it on her own. Save your heroic rescues for the situations that actually require them. Otherwise, you're likely to restrict her growth and confidence later in life.

It's not always easy to do. In fact, it's incredibly hard for me to see my daughter in any amount of pain or discomfort. I absolutely want to save her in those moments, but often times, it's for my ego's fulfillment, not because she actually needs it. I constantly remind myself that her resiliency is more important than my ego, and the lessons she learns from her own rescuing of self will stick with her longer than my rescue. Plus, I won't be there all of the time. Her long-term independence trumps my ego's temporary desires.

I'm not saying we should never help our daughters because we certainly don't want them to feel abandoned or that they can't count on us if needed. My invitation here is to better discern between the times she really needs you to help her and the times YOU need you to help her. Those will be different, and the latter will likely outnumber the former tenfold or more. The best way to think about it is that you are available to her when needed and requested but not always jumping in to solve all her problems.

Julie Lythcott-Haims, former dean of freshman at Stanford University, writes in her book *How to Raise an Adult: Break Free of the Overparenting Trap and Prepare Your Kid for Success* that a lot of depression, antisocial behavior, or other self-harming patterns in college students, including suicide, stem from young adults who don't have confidence in themselves to "do life" because their parents always did everything for them when they were young. I hope that's as sobering to you as it was to me when I first heard it.

Yes, we men love to fix things. When we see problems, we offer solutions, even when they aren't solicited. It's how we are wired and programmed. But if you're always being "Father Fix-It" and taking care of your daughter's problems, she won't learn how to build her own fix-it muscles. Let her make mistakes and prove to herself that she can be strong and independent. Like me, you might have to bite your tongue on occasion as you remind yourself that the future lesson is more important than easing the current discomfort. It's not always easy, but it's possible and worth it.

I recently heard that during the first ten years of our children's lives, we are teaching them how to live with us. But over the next ten years, we should be teaching them how to live *without* us. That really changed the way I think about my role as a "fixer." Since my daughter is well past the age of ten, I'm more focused on helping her be strong and ready for her adult life than I am helping protect her from experiencing any uncomfortable problems.

I'm not talking about physical strength but personal power. I've learned that a lot of girls either grow up believing they are not powerful enough or they are too powerful, and neither one is okay in their minds. Oddly enough, both scenarios can lead to the same outcome—shrinking and shutting down.

Those girls who believe they are not powerful enough may shy away from leadership roles and let others always take the lead. They often won't stand up for themselves and may be taken advantage of in all relationships as a result.

Girls who think they are too powerful will often act the same way because they become afraid of their own power when others appear to be intimidated by it or uncomfortable around it. So they squash it or keep it hidden to "stay in their place" and earn the approval of others. This often leads to depression and/or physical manifestations of emotional suppression.

For instance, autoimmune diseases, especially ones involving the thyroid gland, which is literally wrapped around the windpipe and voice box, are often shown to be correlated with women who are or have been afraid to speak what's on their minds. The fear is usually due to potential repercussions—either being punished or other people feeling bad because of what they say. I have several clients who've reported their thyroid problems basically vanished once they started speaking out more.

Whether there's a proven scientific connection between such diseases and women's fear of power is not the main point here. What's true is that a lot of women don't feel powerful when it comes to voicing their opinions. One way to help avoid that is to always encourage her to speak her mind. Do your best to avoid using shut-down phrases such as *"Because I said so"* or *"I told you to,"* and never, ever say *"children should be seen and not heard."* The lingering effect of those words in adult women years, even decades, later is quite alarming.

Those phrases don't give any explanation, so there isn't any learning that happens. Plus, the overall message is just that you, as the dad, are bigger and older, and therefore, you have the power. Many women take those phrases to mean they don't ever have anything valid to say, that they should always keep their mouth shut, that they are always wrong, or that they don't matter. Again, these are not hypothetical; they are specific experiences with female clients of mine. If you have a disagreement with her, explain why you disagree instead of just using force and a louder volume to win the argument.

There are countless scenarios when these phrases might feel warranted, but they never answer the concerns, they don't teach them how to have healthy disagreements, and they certainly will never leave them feeling empowered. Acknowledge and celebrate her independent thoughts, especially when they differ from yours.

For example, if your daughter is begging for a cookie at bedtime and you say no but she continues to ask, explain your no. Sugar before bed is an unhealthy choice, and you want your daughter to be healthy, so no cookies before bed. If she persists, you can continue to tell her no and explain that you've already told her why. You can also say, "Because I love you and want you to be healthy, safe, successful, and happy." You might be amazed at how well that response lands when it's sincere.

As frustrating as these exchanges may be, you'll cherish her persistence in the future as she grows up, when she's the one saying no to enforce her boundaries or fighting for her own values and beliefs. It's important to allow little girls to be strong with their voice when they're young if you want them to be strong with their voice when they're older. Teach them that it's okay to stand up for themselves as girls so they know how to stand up for themselves as women. You can't shut her confidence down now and expect it to be strong later.

As your girl gets older, this might seem to backfire if she exercises this liberty with you and questions things like, *"Why do I have to be home at ten when my friends can stay out until twelve?"* Just listen and hear her out. Then use the opportunity to explain your perspective and share your heart. Your rule of a ten o'clock curfew is because you love her and want her to be safe at home when it's later at night. She may not like the decision or the rule, but at least she knows why it's in place and that it's coming from love. And, of course, there needs to be flexibility along the way. We should be aware enough to realize that a ten o'clock curfew might be warranted when she's fifteen but not when she's eighteen. Always allow her to negotiate whenever appropriate.

A good analogy to consider is the boundaries of a playpen. When she's little, the boundaries are very close because she doesn't know about the dangers of the world, nor is she capable of figuring them out on her own. But as she grows, her body and mind are not only more capable of learning about the world around, but they are more resilient as well. She can quickly bounce back from the lessons she learns. Our job should be to expand those learning boundaries as she grows and matures in mind and body. In other words, as she becomes more capable, give her more space to roam because her confidence depends on it.

Even if kids don't seem to hear you, their hearts are listening as long as you speak with yours. But if you shut them down, they will continue to shut themselves down. When you can instead be powerful with your essence and vulnerability by speaking from your heart, it will cultivate a healthier relationship, founded on love and respect. Leave your macho ego out of your disagreements. It's dangerous for her self-esteem. (And, really, it's not so good for you either.)

For instance, if there's a conflict or disagreement, keep your voice low and loving. Keep your facial expression neutral or, better yet, smile gently so she knows your love and approval are not being withheld. Keep your body language calm and nonthreatening. A good rule of thumb is to do the exact opposite of what your programmed macho, power-driven tendencies tell you to do.

If your anger wants you to raise your hands, put them into your pockets instead. If your anger wants you to stand up or step toward her, sit down and lean back instead. Don't try to overpower her like a fight between two stubborn rams. She doesn't have horns, and she's not your adversary. She's your little girl who needs you to show her how to learn, how to be independent, and how to disagree with someone she loves without being disempowered or damaging the relationship.

This will teach her how to have healthy relationships as she grows. You don't want your little girl, at any age, to be persuaded by anyone who wants her to do something for them that is not in her best interests, so start early by teaching her it's okay to be strong and stand up for herself. Celebrate her strength and personal power now. You'll sleep easier later in life!

CHAPTER 9

Teach Her How to Use Tools

EVEN THOUGH I ENCOURAGED YOU NOT to be "Father Fix-It," there is some value in you being the masculine teacher and showing her how to use a screwdriver, a saw, and a hammer—maybe even how to change the oil or a flat tire. It helps with her confidence and belief that she has the capability to fend for herself when she needs or wants to.

If you're like me and you're not a great handyman and have to call a plumber to fix the clog in the sink, that's okay. You can still teach basic things, and basic things are better than nothing. The key here is to help your daughter feel empowered by mastering some basic skills that will serve her as she gets older and eventually (gulp) moves out on her own.

Or perhaps, unlike me, you are a good handyman, and you prefer to have her call on you so "Daddy can do it." While that can keep a connection between you, too much of that might teach her to rely on someone else, rather than feeling like she can do things for herself. So whenever possible, include her. Who knows, she might even teach you a thing or two about fixing stuff from her perspective! Be open to that as well. At the very least, let her help you with household projects, so she gets a sense and feeling that she can do it too. Plus, that kind of daddy-daughter time is precious!

Another tool that is important to teach her how to use is her body. My daughter has earned three black belts in Mixed Martial Arts, and the confidence it has given her is priceless. I love it because I know she will be safer in this world with all the skills she has acquired. But your daughter doesn't have to be in advanced martial arts training to learn how to use her body and protect herself. If nothing else, encourage her to take a self-defense class appropriate for her age.

Outside of the classroom, you can teach her how to hold her head up and walk with confidence. When women walk strongly with a purpose, would-be attackers are often intimidated. They prey on weakness, not confidence. Teach her where to kick, punch, or poke men who do attack so she knows the vulnerable spots that will allow her to get loose and get away. If you don't know, take a self-defense class together. Men can be victims too. You won't always be around to protect her, so make sure she can protect herself.

And the most powerful tool you can teach her to use is her mind. Show her how to set goals and create action plans to make them happen. Teach her how to visualize her success, and suggest that she spend time in that space regularly. She will learn this if she sees you doing these activities, so if you're not doing them already, then now is a good time to start. Talk about your goals and your progress as well as your obstacles and how you turn them into opportunities. But do more than talk because...

> Our kids are watching the show, not listening to the lecture.

Anything you can do to help her feel capable is a powerful gift that will pay off later in her life, both for her and for your peace of mind.

CHAPTER 10

Open Your Heart to Her

WE ARE SETTING AN EXAMPLE for our daughters in so many ways. They will not only learn to love as we do but to accept love as we give. We'll dive deeper in a future chapter, but a big piece of every relationship is communication, so let's start there.

Communication can be a complex challenge, but it gets so much easier when we speak from the heart. It's not all about the words you use; it's more about how you say them, what you convey with your body, and the feelings you have behind the words. There are so many ways for communication to go wrong that it's important to make the effort to get it right.

Here are three communication tips that will help.
1. *Never make assumptions.*

2. *Let her hear your heart.*

3. *Learn to love listening.*

First of all, do your best to never make assumptions. Don't assume your daughter knows how you feel about her. Tell her. Show her—over and over and over and over. Don't assume that if you've told her and shown her once she'll always remember it. Emotions are fragile, especially with tender relationships like dads and daughters. Pile it on, even if she seems to resist it, in as many different ways as you can. Be relentless. She needs to know.

If you haven't read *The Five Love Languages* by Dr. Gary Chapman, I highly recommend it. You'll learn how different people express and receive love, and you can improve any relationship by understanding and implementing the principles he shares.

Don't wait for her to ask if you are proud of her. If she's asking, she doesn't know, and I encourage you to be more proactive in letting her know how proud you are of the girl she is, was, and will be.

Remember, when she has Daddy's approval, she is less likely to seek it elsewhere. Tell her what she does that makes you proud, but more importantly, tell her why you're proud of who she is. Even if she doesn't say that it matters, it matters.

My daughter McKenna wrote me this letter, out of the blue, without any knowledge of this book, when she was fourteen years old.

I don't think I tell you enough how much you mean to me. You are always telling me how proud you are of me, and sometimes I didn't believe it, not because I didn't believe you, but because I didn't know exactly why you were proud. But when you said why you were proud of me, and after telling me so many times, I started taking it to heart. Your proudness has stuck with me, but I don't think I told you how much it meant to me to know you are proud of me. Now, whenever I accomplish something, I think of you and how proud you are of me, but more importantly, I think of how proud, lucky, and amazed I am to have a father like you who will love and support me, no matter what. I want you to know that I could never, ever, ever thank you enough for everything you have done for me, whether it was as simple as standing by my side through a problem or watching me go through something painful. You have given me so much great advice about life, and probably still will, but the most important thing you have taught me is, that no matter your age, whether it's a teenager, or a young adult, a parent, or older, have fun in life. Not everything is serious, and you have taught me that a good old belly laugh may be enough to solve problems. I absolutely love laughing with you. I look up and admire how much fun you have with what you do in your job and just in general. I am so, so, so grateful and blessed to have you as my dad. I love you so much. ❤ ❤ ❤ *McKenna*

That letter opened my heart wide, and just typing it here made me cry all over again. I don't share it to brag by any means; I share it to demonstrate that they are watching how we "do life" and listening to everything we tell them. What we say matters, even if it takes a while for our seeds of encouragement to grow.

While we're talking about assumptions, in addition to removing your own, ask your daughter about her assumptions. When we don't understand things, our minds make up meanings, and they are not always meanings that empower or uplift us. Let me share a true story, with different names, to explain how this works.

While in high school, a girl I know named Jenny had a best friend, Trisha. One day, Trisha came to school very upset, with bandages on her wrists. After talking, Jenny found out Trisha had used scissors to slit her wrists. Trisha was hurting, and she did something to try and make that pain go away. Jenny was devastated; she didn't understand why her friend would do such a thing. Trisha was a great student, had a loving family, and was active and successful in sports too. Jenny assumed that she wasn't a good enough friend to Trisha. Otherwise, this never would have happened. The girls talked about it, and Trisha assured Jenny that her actions were no reflection on their relationship.

In adulthood, Jenny had difficulty making close friends, due to the fear of letting them down. It took some deep individual coaching to help her reframe the event to an empowered perspective. Instead of feeling this wouldn't have happened if she had been a better friend, Jenny came to understand that because she was such a strong friend, Trisha felt comfortable enough to take such a drastic action so her friend could help her through a tough time.

This story isn't just about assumptions. Trisha is somebody's daughter who tried to harm herself. Without laying blame on the father specifically, there was something causing enough pain in her life to not only fantasize about but actually make an attempt at ending the pain through suicide. As fathers, we are major factors in our daughters' self-esteem, which has the power to avoid or heal such devastating pain.

And Jenny is somebody's daughter too, who took the actions of someone else to mean she wasn't good enough as a friend. These are the types of real-life scenarios our girls are going to encounter as they forge their way through childhood and into their adult years. The more connected we are to their hearts and the more communication we have with them, the more likely it is that we will notice when they need us to support them through a tough situation. And hopefully, we can teach them that other people's choices or opinions, even those of their closest friends, don't determine their own personal value.

Always ask your daughter about difficult situations in her life. Have critical conversations so she knows you care. Don't let her assume things are a reflection of her in a negative way. Help her see the opportunities that will uplift her by making empowered meanings of events in her life. In other words, if something bad happens to her or around her, it's not her fault and shouldn't decrease how she feels about herself as a person.

During these critical conversations, make every effort to tap into your own heart. You love your daughter, so let your communication always come from that love. If you notice yourself starting to communicate in a way that is not loving, such as reacting with frustration, anger, or even pain, it's important that you read the next two chapters and go through the process to clear what's in your way so you can create loving communication as often as possible.

Your frustration, anger, and pain are not hers to bear, so please don't project them onto her. For instance, a lot of dads will unconsciously bring their work problems home with them and react with anger when their daughters ask innocent questions or just want to spend time together. Often, men will be upset with their boss or frustrated that their favorite team lost again. They may not be able to keep from projecting those negative feelings onto their daughters, who will often internalize them, thinking that they have done something wrong to make Daddy mad again. This is generally unintentional, but the effect is very real.

Trust me, it will cause a lot of emotional damage, some of which is tremendously difficult to undo. Speaking from your heart doesn't mean you are always going to agree or never have difficult conversations. What it means is that you can do those things with love and grace, rather than irritation and disappointment. And you can keep the emotions that are not connected to your daughter out of your relationship with her.

How can you do that? One extremely helpful way is to engage in heart breathing before and during the conversation. The way to do heart breathing is simple: Imagine and then visualize that you are inhaling and exhaling through your heart while trying to breathe with your diaphragm instead of your chest. This small shift forces our brain to focus on our heart, which puts us in a different mindset than regular breathing.

When we put attention on our hearts, we enter a space of love and gratitude, which allows us to be in more control of our emotions and actions. If you're not feeling those emotions from just the breathing, think of the love and gratitude that you have for your daughter, and you'll quickly get there. Then start your conversation from that space. If you notice yourself becoming agitated or irritated, it means you're getting more into your head; do some more heart breathing until you feel grounded again. This practice can be magical when you use it to create more love and connection with your girl.

Search for resources on heart breathing if you want more information. You can also find several free options at HeartMath.org.

Speaking from your heart is simply staying true to your feelings for your daughter and making sure that those feelings are communicated by every word you say. Even if, or when, you are upset with her actions, you still love her as a person. So make sure that feeling is what you tap into when you talk, rather than the upset. You can tell her you're upset, but *say it with love*. Explain what made you upset and why, and reiterate that even though the upset is there, you love her and you are proud of her, no matter what.

While you are connected to your heart, it will be much easier to simply listen. One of the toughest things for many of us men to do, myself included, is to allow someone to talk without jumping in to solve the problems, give our opinions, or critique the situation. When your daughter is talking, listen. Pay attention. Be present. Seek to understand her view of the world, not to fix it. Listen to her words, listen to her heart, listen to her soul. Sometimes, that will be all she needs.

CHAPTER 11

Let Her See You Cry

MEN WHO ALLOW THEMSELVES TO BE emotional are much less likely to be controlling, abusive, or lose their tempers. We are often taught as young boys that crying, or any type of vulnerability, is a sign of weakness to be avoided at all costs. This couldn't be further from the truth. Emotions are a sign of health. We all have them, and our girls need to see that it's okay to be emotionally expressive.

When our daughters feel their own normal and natural emotions, but they've never been taught that it's okay to cry, the only thing they have left to do is bottle it all up inside themselves. This is typically what men do with their emotions, anyway, so we teach our girls that it's the only way to be "strong." This is an incredibly damaging pattern that we men have endured and perpetuated for far too long.

Please allow me to take us down a rabbit hole for a moment, to explore our masculine programming. I think there's a significant reason that most random acts of violence are performed by men. Let's look at the extreme example of all the mass shootings in the United States. I certainly haven't studied all of these incidents, but as a criminal justice major, I've always been fascinated by these kinds of end-of-the-spectrum crimes. I constantly seek to understand what psychological factors contribute to the most excessively deviant and deplorable human behavior.

These random shootings are generally carried out by white men who are lower middle class and above. I'm speaking in generalities, of course, just for the purposes of this discussion on emotions, not to make any other type of racial or political statements. The relevant point is that these shooters are not committing the crimes for some sort of tangible personal gain, such as money or status, things that drive most criminals. They are killing people for a minuscule, temporary experience of power, knowing full well that it won't last because they will either be jailed, killed, or commit suicide. So, what causes someone to make that ridiculously irrational choice?

In my estimation, these men are emotional powder kegs who feel helpless, hopeless, and unable to control their rage after years and years of either real or perceived neglect, abandonment, violence, and other traumas. No rational, healthy person would ever make this decision. These are power-driven acts of desperation perpetrated by men who have lost control of their anger, anxiety, and fears.

These mass shooters are certainly not vulnerable men who are comfortable with expressing their emotions and getting support from others.

By most accounts, they are carrying a lot of shame inside, which is one of the worst feelings men can experience and most often a result of emotional suppression. Usually, it is discovered that the perpetrators have severe emotional disconnections in their families, especially with their fathers.

The pure masculine energy is committed to protecting human life, both itself and others, never taking human life unless in self-defense. So these men are so disconnected from their innate masculine tendencies that they act in complete opposition to their natural instincts. Furthermore, many of the shooters who didn't kill themselves later say if someone would have just listened to their struggles, it would have all been avoided.

Another extreme example is the difference in suicide rates among men and women. While women are more likely to attempt suicide, men are far more likely to be successful because they tend to use more definitively lethal means, such as guns, hanging, jumping, etc. When a man's shame and emasculation have reached an intolerable level, he tends to turn that deadly rage of wounded masculinity on himself, others, or both. The common perception that men don't have a safe space to be vulnerable, especially with other men, is something that affects all of us.

While the men in these examples become suicidal and/or homicidal, millions and millions of us, every day, are making less egregious but still unhealthy and harmful choices from losing this exact same internal battle with our emotions. This is the dire situation I'm committed to addressing. I don't believe any infant boy is born destined to be a bully, criminal, or mass murderer. I think they are created by a recipe of trauma and overwhelmingly negative experiences that culminate into an eruption of violent rage. If we treat this discussion as a collective problem, a journey we all walk, then we can dissect it for all of ourselves, regardless of the intensity of the details that any of us are uniquely dealing with.

Boiled down to its essence, the simple problem is men not being able or willing to manage their emotions. We've all fought that battle to some degree, and it's a battle we can absolutely win if we know how and if we have a big enough thing to fight for. I'm hoping your daughter fits that last condition.

To some, going from braiding hair to suicide and mass shootings might seem unnecessary, but it's relevant because it speaks to the reality of how men often feel incapable of dealing with pent-up emotions of weakness and vulnerability. Instead of looking at all the crimes men commit as separate acts with separate variables, let's imagine a single continuum representing men's relationship to their emotions. With that as the basis, the varying coping behaviors men choose are the byproducts of not managing their feelings and actions. This applies to all of us.

I'm in no way trying to justify those acts or sympathize with the criminals. I'm only looking at the emotional landscape for most adult men, which is not a very kind or safe one. How well do we deal with our own emotions? And, if we don't do it well, who else is affected as a result?

My experience tells me that everyone around us is affected, and our daughters' relationship with emotions can be forever damaged if they don't see and experience our male vulnerability.

First, they won't know how to deal with their own emotions. If they haven't seen a model of how to express emotions in a healthy way, they will only follow what they've seen. Whether this is taught explicitly or not, the message is that emotions themselves are not approved of, and therefore, anyone who has emotions is also not going to be approved of.

Remember how powerful your daughter's desire is to be approved of by you. She wants you to be proud and never wants to disappoint you. Even if she sees her mom being a little better at expressing her emotions, she's still wanting approval from her dad and will suppress her feelings as best she can to achieve it if she believes that's the established rule. Your actions will communicate what's okay for her to do and not do in order to gain or keep your approval. In short, she thinks what you do is "okay" and what you don't do clearly is "not okay."

The influence of modeling parental behavior is immense in young children, and they keep operating on those lessons for the rest of their lives unless, and until, they are intentionally changed. Even if your daughter is well beyond that influential time period, the lessons she learned and decisions she made during those years are still with her today. And the great news is that anything that was learned can be unlearned, so it's never too late to help her make healthy internal shifts.

Second, we want our daughters to believe that men can be safe when they get emotional. I can't stress enough the fact that so many women have literally never been in the presence of healthy, transparent, emotional masculinity that doesn't seek to harm or hush them. Unfortunately, that emotionally healthy man is a very rare animal who doesn't get to see the light of day very often. Therefore, many women don't believe he actually exists. As her dad, you can show her, not just tell her, that she can trust being in the presence of an emotionally expressive man who seeks connection instead of domination.

The main point to all of this is to learn how to freely express and manage your emotions for your own happiness and sanity and for what you'll teach your daughter in the process. In order to actualize itself, the feminine energy in our daughters needs to trust the power of healthy masculinity. These are not two opposing forces at war with each other. In reality, the masculine and feminine need and strengthen each other when they are in their healthy forms.

What I mean is that when the feminine energy, which is much more passive and open, does not feel safe around masculine energy because it's afraid of being hurt by it again, the feminine will retreat into the shadows to be safe. Therefore, it never fully develops itself, nor does it develop its relationship with the masculine energy. As a result, the masculine never experiences the healthy support from the feminine energy, and it, therefore, doesn't develop fully either. So these two energies become suspicious of or threatened by each other, creating a rivalrous relationship when they aren't truly rivals.

You are your daughter's first and most significant experience of masculine energy. Well before she can put it into words or comprehend it consciously, she decides whether the masculine, men specifically, is safe, loving, and trustworthy. Later in life, when she is confronted with unhealthy or toxic masculinity, she will see it as abnormal compared to what you showed her because yours will always be the gold standard to which all others are compared.

But if she never sees the healthy form, as is the case for many women, she will believe the dangerous type is the *only* type. Her only choice will be how to protect herself from it, rather than how to discern between healthy and unhealthy men. This is also one of the reasons why many women either don't recognize healthy men or they are suspicious of them because they've never been introduced to one. Please, be that one for her.

For the most part, all of this simply means being emotionally expressive as a human being. There's nothing you need to learn how to do, nor or there any skills you are missing. It's all about permission. You must be willing to allow your emotions to be what they are instead of trying to suppress them. They are naturally occurring human experiences. The hard part is going against the grain of our male programming, which essentially taught us that emotions are the epitome of weakness, especially for us macho men.

All that being said, I'm not asserting that you need to force crying just for the sake of crying. Although nearly all of us have uncried tears we never allowed to come out, not everyone needs to cry. If it's not there, it's not there, and that's fine. But don't be afraid of crying either. That's the key distinction.

Most men have never had a safe place to be emotionally expressive, so we don't allow it. If you're touched by something, allow your emotions to be felt and (deep breath) seen by others. Specifically, share them with your daughter. Let her see you be real. You will not lose your masculinity, toughness, or your authority in any way. In fact, they will be increased in her eyes. Trust me.

Vulnerable masculinity is so rarely seen or felt, but it *is* the answer to so many of our problems as men, and society in general, both internally and externally. It essentially does the work on its own. It is a self-healing and self-actualizing entity of energy. It just needs to be let out, which is often the scariest thing a man can do because of the lies we've been told throughout our lives. We weren't just taught that it was weak, we were taught in no uncertain terms that we would be shunned by the men in our lives if we ever let it out. *"Don't cry," "Don't be a little girl," "Suck it up," "Walk it off," "Be a man,"* or *"Don't be a pussy."*

I'm sure those sound very familiar. The underlying message is if you are emotional, you are not a real man and will not belong to the tribe of men that we so desperately want to belong to. The fear of being ostracized by our own team, if you will, is enough to cause most of us to deny our natural tendencies and stuff our emotions until it becomes our norm. We'll do whatever we think they want us to do to gain or keep our belonging. It's time to break this pattern, for ourselves and our daughters.

Vulnerability is also not only about crying. You don't have to cry to be transparent. In fact, vulnerability is not about *doing* anything. Vulnerability is—*being*. Being real. Being authentic. Being present. Being human—without trying to defend or pretend. Transparently share your fears and doubts and worries with your daughter, whenever and wherever appropriate. Basically, show her your heart and your humanity. She'll learn that it's okay to not only have those normal human emotions since her dad does, too, but also to share them with others so she doesn't keep them building up inside of herself.

My family has seen me cry at movies, TV shows, and feel-good videos. When our family cat Peter died, I cried so hard. He was my guy. We got him before we had our kids, and I used him to propose to Cybil by putting the engagement ring around his collar until she found it on her own. Just typing that made me tear up a little. He was my favorite pet ever. In the grieving room at the vet, we all talked as a family about fond memories and allowed ourselves to be sad that those times were at an end. It was the first family loss for our kids, and I know the collective tears brought us together inside our sadness.

One year later, I cried much louder and much harder when my dad died of pancreatic cancer after living with us for his final eighty days. Another year later, I cried guttural tears of grief and shame as my mother died with me being the only one left in her hospital room, hours after we pulled her off life support. I believe that some of the deepest and most valuable experiences in life *require* tears to flow. While it might feel uncomfortable or awkward in the beginning, opening your emotional channel will eventually be liberating emotionally and even physically. It will lift a weight off your shoulders and allow you to be more grounded in your life, in all ways. It won't always be fun, but it will be powerful.

My crying lets my daughter know that it's okay to be sad and express her own sadness too. Being vulnerable does not take any strength away or diminish your manhood. Especially as fathers, our families are watching and learning from us how to emotionally deal with death, grief, or anything else that pulls at our heartstrings. Don't hide that powerful lesson. Teach it openly.

If you were brought up with phrases like, "*Dry those tears,*" or "*Stop being a baby,*" or one of my favorites, "*I'll give you something to cry about,*" please don't pass those on to your daughters (or sons either). I understand our parents were doing the best they could, and they meant well and were likely at the end of their ropes when they uttered those words. But they just conveyed that being emotional, one of the beautiful and unique ingredients of being human, isn't okay.

The truth is that those sentiments identify people who are uncomfortable with their own vulnerability toward crying, so when they see it in someone else, they want to put a stop to it. It's an overall fear that most of society has toward vulnerability that needs to change if we are going to heal some of the problems we have inside ourselves and our relationships with those around us.

CHAPTER 12

Master Your Emotions

MOST MEN ARE MASTERED *by* their emotions, rather than masters *of* their emotions. Emotions are normal human sensations we experience in relation to events in our lives. It's that simple: nothing more and nothing less. Having and expressing emotions doesn't make you any less of a man. In fact, it makes you more POWERFUL as a man because you are in control. When we're afraid of them, they control us.

It's important to understand that we have the power to choose our emotional experiences. Of course, our behaviors have been programmed since birth by a multitude of memories, and we react to events so quickly that it doesn't often seem like we have a choice, but we do.

Holding your emotions in—good or bad—is not healthy. Emotions are *energy in motion*. If you stop the movement of energy, you block the flow of life. Being emotional is one of the sacred human experiences; allow the energy to flow through you in order to have more internal control.

My life was changed in large part by Jack Canfield's work on this topic, something I now call the Six Layers of Human Emotion. It has become a staple of my work. These six layers are:

1. Anger
2. Pain
3. Fear
4. Regret
5. Desire
6. Love

Of course, we have many more labels for so many other emotions, but all of them can be categorized into these main six. I've found this simple framework to be extremely useful and practical to implement for myself personally, as well as with my clients. Here's how it works:

Think of each layer as a different story of a building. Love is at the bottom; it's the foundation, with all the other stories above it. Therefore, in order for one of the higher-level emotions to exist, there must be lower emotions beneath it.

For instance, the only way for regret to be present is if there is also desire and love. In other words, you won't hold onto any regret around something you never cared about.

Similarly, if you are angry, underneath all the anger is pain, fear, regret, desire, and love. All of them must be present, like ingredients in a recipe. It can be tough to admit or even be aware of those other emotions, but that's where the profound power lies. It's worth it to put this model to use and begin to untie our emotional knots.

The way to control your emotions is to acknowledge and express the ones below the one you are feeling. Like letting the air out of a tire, the more we release the energy of the lower emotions, the less pressure there is inside the higher emotions and the less likely they are to "pop" uncontrollably and dangerously.

Plus, when you explore the lower emotions, you will often find the answers to actually get rid of the anger altogether—or at the very least, dissipate the overinflation of it. There's nothing wrong with these emotions; they are all natural. The problem is when the anger released is not proportional to the situation, such as a massive emotional blowup over a minor incident of miscommunication.

I liken it to us carrying around a huge bag, like Santa's gigantic gift sack, of repressed emotions. But let's be clear, we are not carrying around any gifts for other people! When our anger gets triggered, we tend to release all the rage from the sack that we've been carrying around for years and years and years. So the response is not proportional to the situation.

That's why many parents will erupt on their kids when the "offense" is relatively minor. And neither the kid nor the parent understands what just happened. The sadness in this scenario is that the majority of the anger that gets thrown onto the children has nothing to do with them. It's all unexpressed, trapped emotions from the past.

This is also precisely why so many women are afraid of a man's emotions being released—they have been in the blast zone before and felt the horrible impact. That's the experience they then try to protect themselves from for the rest of their lives. They unconsciously decide that all emotions = dangerous emotions, which they apply to the emotions in themselves as well as others.

To run with this analogy, imagine that giant emotional sack is full of sand. First of all, it's extremely heavy to haul around! That's how so many of us men experience our emotions. They are exhausting to keep carrying, which shortens our tempers even further.

The best way to ease this heavy burden is to poke a small hole in the sack and let the sand start to ooze out on its own, using the force of gravity. And then poke another hole, and another, and another. Pretty soon, the sack will empty without much effort on your part.

But our egos don't want anybody else to see us leaking sand. Again, our macho programming says it's a weakness. We usually find more value in how much sand we can carry, a sign of toughness and strength, than how much sand we can release. But in reality, carrying around all that heaviness causes more physical and emotional weakness than letting it out. And it endangers the ones we love with our emotional outbursts, should they be in the blast zone when we erupt.

Poking holes in the sack of sand is the equivalent of expressing your emotions so they release from your body. And just like the sand seeps out without effort, our emotions also want to be let out. Emotions are energy that want to be in motion, not trapped. It doesn't take effort to release them, only permission from our egos.

Instead of wrestling with your machismo about what it means

to leak sand, remind yourself what it means to lighten your load and that everyone around you will be spared from all the heavy sand that isn't theirs to bear.

If we apply the Six Layers of Human Emotion concept to the analogy, instead of one huge sack of sand with all the emotions mixed together, imagine you're carrying six separate sacks, one for each of the emotions, each holding a separate color of sand.

Anger = Red
Pain = Brown
Fear = Blue
Regret = Green
Desire = Yellow
Love = White

When all the emotions are swirling together, it's very difficult to identify or control them. Just imagine trying to pick out each of the different colors of sand grains when they're all mixed together in the huge sack. Thankfully, in real life, each emotion is very different from the others and can be isolated with intention and practice.

So instead of poking a random hole in the huge sack of sand (I call it our SOS), it's more helpful to find the targeted individual emotion and poke a hole into the smaller, individual sack. This type of isolated expression, much like isolating individual muscles in the gym, is the best way to gain control over our emotional states. But this isn't the way most of us were taught to deal with the emotions that we're not even supposed to have in the first place. No wonder there's so much confusion and difficulty when it comes to our internal control.

Now, let's take a look at an important distinction in this hierarchy, between the top four and the bottom two.

Love and *desire* are the natural states when we are born, which is why they are at the bottom and all the others lie on top of them. They are much lighter and more flowing in their energy. I represent them with two of the lightest colors, white and yellow.

The top four are constructed through experiences when we feel deprived of the bottom two. The higher the layer, the more intensity that emotion usually has. And when the main deprived desire is to be loved, the intensity is exaggerated even further.

Even though the existence of the top four emotions is not "bad," the effects of them generally are, especially for men. So although it's normal and natural to feel anger, pain, fear, and regret, we often behave with negative consequences because of those feelings. We tend to destroy our circumstances and relationships by tearing them down when we are controlled by the emotions. Because of that, I refer to them as the Destructive Four.

When we are present to and communicate from love and desire, however, we tend to build up our circumstances and relationships in healthy ways. I refer to these two as the Constructive Core because they are the internal foundation of emotional health.

Now let's dissect each emotion individually and see how they lead to the ones above, beginning with the lowest layer of the Destructive Four.

Regret is a sadness created after the disappointment of one or more of our desires not being met. It is based in the past.

Fear is an anxiety created when we imagine one of our desires might not be met in the future, remembering the regret that results from that happening. Because fear is constructed in the unknown future, it can quickly become irrational and uncontrollable, like chasing ghosts.

Pain is the experience of losing one of our desires that we already possessed, either in reality or in our imagination. It often feels like something was literally ripped away from us, and therefore, our pain is stored in the cells of our bodies until it gets released.

Most men have this kind of pain that hasn't been grieved properly. These are the uncried tears that weigh so heavily on us, both psychologically and emotionally. That pain is generally some form of abandonment, lack of nurturing from our parents or other parental figures, or the memory of our poor performance in important situations. Sometimes it's a specific single incident, such as our dad forgetting to pick us up from hockey practice one day and we spent hours walking home, wondering if he was going to come get us (feeling forgotten and unimportant, etc.).

More often, it's from a collection of many circumstances or incidents, such as never feeling supported or valued in our childhood, being used as a pawn during our parents' divorce, never being allowed to show emotions, etc. The performance pain could be the jump shot we missed at the buzzer, getting laughed at in front of the classroom, or asking our first crush out on a date and getting rejected.

Whether we consciously remember any of this or not, it's the fundamental journey of human evolution during childhood. We all experienced this kind of emotional upset to some degree or another. It's impossible not to, unless every single experience went exactly according to your desires as you grew up. I think it's safe to assume that the next person who fits that description will be the first ever.

All of those individual experiences are traumatic to our growing minds at different intensity levels. Some are very painful, which I call *macro*traumas. Others are shallower, which I call *micro*traumas. All together, they form an internal reservoir of uncried tears that, over time, becomes more and more pressurized.

Females are programmed by our society that it's okay to have and express these tears. Males are programmed with the exact opposite message. Not only are we not supposed to express them, we aren't even supposed to *have* them. Yet, we all do.

Some men are so committed to not feeling their emotions that they detach from themselves to such an extreme, they literally become psychopathic and/or sociopathic. These individuals have become so disconnected from their humanity that they lack empathy for others, and therefore, have no problem inflicting pain and suffering, even on people they love.

These are the mass shooters, the serial killers, the professional criminals, the human traffickers, the serial rapists, the violent racists, the hardcore gang members, etc. Lower on the same spectrum are the abusers, the kidnappers, the narcissists, the thieves, the bullies, and the like. For the most part, it's the same projection of pain onto others but at different levels of intimacy and intensity. It all falls under what I call the "masculine wound"—hurt people who are hurting people. This pattern of violence toward others is much more predominant in men.

In my opinion and experience as a life coach, there is a clear correlation between emotional expression and empathy. The less connected we are to our own humanity, the less connected we are to others' humanity, and vice versa. Thankfully, most men don't get all the way to the wrong extreme of that empathy spectrum, but the lower level gradients of that path can and will generally be devastating nonetheless.

Here's another metaphor that might land better for some people. Imagine a towel slowly absorbing drops of liquid one at a time. While the effect of each drop of liquid might be unnoticeable, at some point the weight of that towel has increased dramatically from its natural state. And there's a threshold where it simply cannot absorb any more liquid until it gets wrung out. Essentially, the towel has become unstable, having reached its breaking point.

Unfortunately, that's how so many of us men live our lives. We're the towels, and the liquid represents all the emotions we've absorbed along the way. And if we're afraid to wring out the towel by expressing our pain and other feelings, the only alternative is to constantly protect our saturated towel from touching any more liquid or being touched by anyone or anything that might cause it to start leaking "weakness." That is exhausting and puts us in a constant state of protection and anxiety.

Back to the dissection of emotions, we still have the top layer of the Destructive Four to discuss—*anger*. Anger is the dangerous and highly unstable culmination of all of this. It's the ultimate attempt to protect ourselves from any more liquid because we're desperately afraid of feeling the pain and not being able to make it stop. We're also afraid of losing our sense of strength—in our own eyes and in the eyes of others.

When our masculine identity is at risk of being lost, the anger is at its greatest because the perceived danger is so high, which is essentially the loss of our self-image as a man. The more imminent the danger, the more desperate the anger. The root of desperation is despair, which is the complete loss or absence of hope. That's what the anger is trying to protect us from feeling and why it can get so vicious at times. It behaves as though it is under attack, so it attacks back.

When the threat of despair feels real, the anger turns to rage and often violence. It's a barbaric, kill-or-be-killed, primal state of mind, operating as though our survival is at stake. Even though our literal survival is not being threatened, our self-image is. So, to some degree, the threat is indeed existential in nature, as it threatens death to our wounded, masculine ego. Desperate to be perceived as strong and competent by ourselves and those around us, we strike out to thwart the attack. This is how so many of us men are living. It's not fun. It's not healthy. It's utterly debilitating.

Instead of existing in this constant high alert, high danger, high tension state of being, it's *much* better to release the pressure through emotional expression. With a better understanding of how these feelings are operating in conjunction with each other, you will have more control in all situations, whether you're dealing with your own behavior or the behavior of others. It works like magic, and I'm a living testament. Let's explore my journey as a case study.

Not so long ago, I carried around my own gigantic sack of emotions with an explosive concoction of the Destructive Four.

Even though I've always been fairly mellow and my anger rarely got triggered, when it did, it was deep. And dangerous.

I never threw my emotions onto my wife or kids in an aggressive way, but I would punch walls, break things around the house, and yell out in anger over the most ridiculous incidents, like my favorite sports team losing a game, or playing poorly during a win, or even missing a single, meaningless shot.

I remember one time Kobe Bryant of the Los Angeles Lakers missed a jump shot to lose a basketball game. It wasn't even the playoffs, just a regular season game. I erupted.

I threw whatever was in my hand at the time against the wall, screamed at the TV, and paced around the room, lost in a temper tantrum. I couldn't control my feelings and felt like I wanted to break something, so I told my wife I was going for a run. I'm not a runner, I actually hated running, so this wasn't normal at all. But I needed to let this anger out.

Now, of course, that was a better decision than taking it out on my family members or causing expensive damage to the house, but my wife and young kids watched Dad lose his temper like a child and abandon them for the rest of the evening. Who knows what connections they made that night? But it wasn't a healthy display of how to handle losing.

In my younger days, however, I was aggressive externally. I projected my anger onto my mom with verbal abuse, as though she had to pay for my pain. I hate admitting this, but the truth is that I bullied her the majority of my teenage and young adult years.

Like a mean game of emotional hot potato, I intentionally caused her a lot of pain to try to mask the existence of my own. And, of course, that never heals the pain, which is why it is a perpetual cycle that many of us men are in. It wasn't until many years later, when I applied this exact framework of emotions into my life, that I gained empathy for my mom and stopped hurting her.

In fact, this was such a powerful revelation for me that I wrote and performed a one-man play about my relationship with her and the ultimate healing I found through emotional release and self-forgiveness. If this resonates with you on any level, you can access the full play via the link at the back of the book.

If I look at the Six Layers of Human Emotion framework, from the top down, here's the condensed truth.

Anger. I was angry at my mom because she smoked, she didn't work, she was in counseling, she didn't go to all of my baseball games, and she didn't have our family sense of humor.

Pain. Underneath the anger, I felt the pain of abandonment as I judged my mom's many "offenses" through the perspective of her not nurturing and loving me. All of those memories of her not giving me what I wanted lived in the cells of my body.

Fear. Underneath the pain was fear of never getting what I actually wanted, which was for her to be the perfect mom, according to my impossible standards.

Regret. Underneath the fear was regret that we didn't have a loving relationship, and the personal regret of all the mean things I said to her, and all the times I pushed her away—all the defense mechanisms I built up to keep her out of my heart. After I peeled the top layers away, I was able to see that I played a significant part in the broken relationship. But we are rarely able to see our own responsibility while we're being controlled by those four destructive emotions. Until we acknowledge our individual responsibility, we cannot change the situation in a healthy way.

Desire. Underneath all of that destructive protection, I desired a better relationship with the woman who gave birth to me, the only mom I will ever have.

Love. And underneath all of that was pure love for this woman, the same lady I wanted to marry when I was a small child and believed was perfect in all ways. The depth of the love often mirrors the intensity of the anger but at a deeper level of awareness that most of us haven't opened yet.

I'm sure your personal details are either slightly or radically different than my details, but the way your emotions stack on top of each other is virtually the same, especially for men who've endured the same type of societal programming about what's right and wrong for us to feel and express.

Okay, let's put all these concepts into practical application. First, let's apply it to your own emotional management. Whenever you notice you are experiencing one of the Destructive Four emotions, look to identify and express the feelings beneath it.

If you feel angry, first express the anger in a healthy way. Punch a pillow, yell (not at anybody), clench your muscles, go to the gym, do fifty pushups, write it all out in a journal, or express it verbally to someone in a nonthreatening way by simply saying *"I'm angry because..."*

I always suggest doing something physical and verbal, either spoken or written word because together they dislodge the intense energy as well as give voice to acknowledge the anger, which has a vibration to it. If you put your hand anywhere on your throat and say something out loud, you will feel the vibrations moving through your body as it comes out of your mouth. This vibrational release doesn't happen when you keep it all inside your head.

Think of it this way...

> If you never express your anger, where does it go?

The answer is that it stays inside the body, wanting to be released, festering, pressurizing, and creating more and more tension until one of two things occurs—a safe expression or a dangerous explosion.

Make sure you don't yell *at* anyone in the anger expression. I know you and I were yelled at as boys, whether it was at home, or on our sports teams, or in the classroom, or on the playground. And I know that society condones and endorses yelling in so many ways through the media and what we promote in our culture.

However, in the history of human existence, it has yet to be proved that yelling at people ever solves anything in a healthy way or makes anybody feel good. Remember, the premise of this book is the protection of self-esteem, specifically in our girls. Screaming and yelling cannot do that.

Yelling absolutely works to shut people down and influence behavior with threats, like a caged lion being whipped by the trainer. But it's never empowering; it never produces trust, happiness, or learning, nor is it ever required.

We, as men, need to rise above our programming and propensity to yell by tapping into our vulnerable, stable, and authentic masculinity. When we find this deeply rooted source of presence and power, we will no longer feel the need for the illusions of strength, such as raising our voice to control people. And we will actually accomplish what we want to accomplish much easier.

> Yelling is a sign of insecurity, not strength.

Once the anger has been expressed and given a voice (imagine the red sand leaking from the anger sack), take a deep, calming breath, like downshifting in a car, and ask yourself, "*What pain is underneath the anger?*" Similar to a pile of blankets, once the top one has been removed, the one below it is now accessible. Emotions work the same way. I call this process "isolate and express." We want to work with different emotions one at a time. Otherwise, it's like herding frightened cats.

As soon as you identify and connect with the pain, your physical energy will shift slightly or significantly because anger and pain operate differently in the body. If the pain is something you can solve in that moment, solve it. If you feel like crying, cry. Often, nothing really needs to be done, we just need to experience the sensation of the emotion for it to flow out of our body on its own. Now the brown sand is leaking from the pain sack.

Next, downshift with a deep breath and ask yourself, *"What am I afraid of?"* Keep in mind that most of our fears will never happen. Or if they do happen, they won't be nearly as bad as we were imagining. Just the identification of the fear will again shift your energy and usually cause you to feel more in control, as ironic as that may sound. I suggest using the following questions to confront your fears.

1. *What are the chances that this negative outcome actually happens?*
2. *If it happens, how bad will it really be?*
3. *If it's really bad, how temporary is it?*

Most of our fears won't make it through all three questions before we realize that it would be silly to give much power to that particular fear. But sometimes the fear is of something that really is likely, potentially very bad, and permanent. In that case, take the necessary precautions to avoid the disaster. But generally, the blue sand will just start falling and the fear will diminish, maybe even dissolve completely.

Next, downshift with a deep breath, and ask yourself, *"What do I regret?"* Sometimes this will be an action that was or wasn't taken by you or somebody else, or it will be a situation. For example, you can regret not being present at a birthday party, or you can regret the tension in a relationship.

Either way, noticing what you regret will usually give you something to take action on. If you regret words you said to someone, apologize. If you regret that somebody didn't attend your wedding, tell them. If you regret the status of a relationship, take the responsibility to change it however you can. Since regret is generally the perception that something is or was "wrong," you will usually be able to either make it right or, at the very least, express your feelings about it being wrong. The green sand is now leaking out of its sack.

At this point, notice what has happened in the process. The four destructive emotions are being drained, making everything lighter and easier to carry. And you're now in some type of motion, giving you the sense of choice and control. You've made massive progress away from the angry state, even if you were to stop here. But, let's continue.

Once the Destructive Four have been expressed, you have healthy access to your lower two levels of emotion without the weight and cloudiness of the other layers pressing down from above. When you breathe deeply now, it will feel more like you have "dropped into" your heart's desires. From this place, ask yourself, *"What do I really want?"* You'll feel it differently, and you'll be able to express them clearly to the people who can help you fulfill them. Plus, you will be more likely to actually experience what you wanted all along.

Unlike the Destructive Four emotions, the yellow sand of your desires doesn't leak from the sack. Rather, it is revealed and more accessible to you. You will have a much healthier connection to your true wants without the resistance or shame from the layers above.

Finally, with one more deep breath, ask yourself, *"Who or what do I truly love?"* You will be more connected to your experience of and capacity to share love. You will feel more calm, relaxed, and alive. You will be coming from a place of true strength and control. You will feel more connected to your body, even if it feels massively foreign and uncomfortable. And everyone, especially your daughter, will be able to feel and benefit from it.

Again, the white sand does not fall from its sack. It actually begins to expand into all the areas of your life, infusing you and your relationships with the healthiest and most powerful force we can experience as humans: unveiled love.

This process flat-out works, but it is definitely a new pattern that often needs to be practiced multiple times before it takes hold as a habit. So, if you experience some challenges, or you don't feel like you did it right, or aren't experiencing what I said you would, don't worry. It sometimes can be difficult to take ourselves through a brand-new process on our own, especially an emotional one, without the support and guidance of someone with an external perspective. If you find yourself struggling, there are quite a few resources in the back of this book that I encourage you to plug into. In all my years as a coach, I've never met anybody who isn't able to do this work (when they have the right support and guidance), only people who aren't willing to. If you're willing, it can be done.

Now that we understand what's happening inside ourselves with our emotions, we know what's happening inside everyone else as well because it's virtually the same. Males and females have similar experiences of emotions in this hierarchy, but the way we are programmed to express them varies greatly.

When your daughter is angry, apply this same awareness of what's really happening underneath her behavior, and you'll be able to see the lower levels of her emotions as well, which is not only very cool to witness but an incredibly valuable tool to help her grow emotionally healthy.

As she gets older and more expressive or confrontational with her anger, you will be able to remain calmer as you see your little girl for her pain and fear, rather than meeting her anger with your own. When two angry people confront each other, there's usually going to be two different versions of "loss." One person loses the battle, while the other person loses control in order to win the battle. And generally, neither one of them walks away feeling good or empowered.

I frequently tell my clients to "speak to their lower levels of emotion" to dissipate anger in others. What I mean by that is to speak to your daughter's pain, fear, regret, desires, or love, whichever is appropriate in the moment. You don't have to educate her on any of this to speak to her lower levels.

For example, I once had a client who was going through a potential divorce from her husband, and her teenage daughter was extremely angry at her for breaking up the family by having an affair. She did not actually have an affair or anything close to one, but her husband was wrongly accusing her of being unfaithful so their daughter would side with him during the breakup. As you might imagine, my client was infuriated at the false accusations and felt betrayed by both her daughter and husband. She called me to help her through this mess.

I took her through this process of identifying and expressing these Six Layers of Human Emotion, but from her daughter's perspective. What stood out the most was her daughter's fear that if the family broke up, her mom would abandon her. So, I told my client to speak to her daughter's fear, rather than engage her anger the next time her daughter went on the attack.

The next day, I got a call from my client saying that her daughter started screaming at her the night before, as usual. But instead of screaming back and denying her allegations in a rage-filled counter-attack, she calmly said, "*No matter what happens between your father and me, I'm never leaving you.*" (She spoke directly to the fear of her mother's abandonment, without addressing or explaining it explicitly.)

Immediately, her daughter broke down crying, her anger dissolved into sadness, and they were able to share a powerful moment between a mother and daughter through love and connection, rather than anger. I am crying as I type these words now, remembering that moment and what kind of healing this work can produce among loved ones.

You will find that your responses at the lower levels of emotion will be gentler and the whole experience of conflict communication will be more productive and positive for both of you. As she gets older, teach your daughter this framework so she can understand her own emotional makeup and control her communication intentionally. You might want to start with this quote…

Emotions buried alive never die.

Your daughter needs to know how to handle her own anger, pain, fear, regret, and frustration in general, so don't stuff those emotions inside, trying to hide them on the premise of protecting her. She'll just learn to eat those emotions as well, either figuratively or literally with unhealthy foods, and she'll likely create any number of negative coping habits as a result.

When you make the effort to work through the layers of emotion, you'll be releasing them from your energy and your physical body, putting yourself in more control of your actions and behaviors to be a better father. Plus, you're modeling it for your whole family. This modeling is critical for our daughters to see so they know it's okay for them to be emotional themselves and learn how to express their emotions in a productive way. If it's okay for dad, it must be okay for her too!

CHAPTER 13

Clear Your Pain

I WANT TO DIVE A LITTLE DEEPER into what I believe is the biggest problem for men—stuffed pain. Anger is what we see on the surface and what fuels the destructive behaviors, but it's not the root problem. Pain is.

In my experience, pain is the heaviest emotion we carry as men. Especially when we place shame on top of the pain because of what it supposedly says about our manhood if we let on that we've been hurt or admit we are incapable of providing, protecting, or performing. It's crippling to our egos. But it doesn't have to stay that way.

Because of our programming, we are essentially taught to play whack-a-mole with all this pain. Remember that carnival game where plastic moles pop their heads up from their holes and we get points for whacking them with our big stuffed hammer?

Tons of fun—for a carnival. But it's not how we should try to manage our pain. Although some masculine environments will give us points, in the form of status or respect, for pushing our emotions down, it's an unhealthy way to deal with real life.

Let me make something clear. All this talk about being open with your emotions does *not* mean you will be a blubbering pile of mush whenever your emotions get triggered. Actually, it's the opposite. The more open you are with them, the less you'll fear them and the more you can eventually control them, even if it takes a little bit of time.

There are plenty of situations where it wouldn't be productive for you to start "leaking" tears. For instance, you might be in a leadership scenario where you are leading a group of people in the middle of some type of conflict, whether it be in sports competition, the corporate boardroom, public service, etc.

The last thing a team of any type needs to see is their leader seemingly breaking under pressure. In those situations, you most definitely need to be bold and certain in your leadership for everyone's best interest.

This type of emotional work will actually *enhance* your ability to do exactly that and maintain control when you need to because you'll understand the triggers and be able to control your responses. Plus (and this part is huge), you won't have all the extra sandbags ready to burst inappropriately. *That* is the real pressure that most men break under—the emotional weight they're *already* carrying, not the weight of the current moment.

If you haven't started releasing the excess baggage, you are energetically running away from your problems, while simultaneously hauling them around everywhere you go. Essentially, by avoiding them you're telling yourself that you can't handle them, which adds a good helping of shame to the recipe.

Men tend to crack and fold when it looks like they are going to finally succumb to the emotions they've been running from for so long. If that's true for you, you'll never be able to focus on just the situation at hand because you are battling your past and your present at the same time.

We've all been there, we've all tried that, and nobody has ever lived a healthier or happier life that way. Without all the built-up pressure from the past, you'll be present with the current situation with a clear head, giving you easier access to your wisdom and making it more likely for you to make the best decisions in the moment. You'll notice your confidence increase in the process, and you might just astound yourself with what you're capable of without all the pressure and fatigue from the emotional baggage.

Hurt people hurt people.

In my coaching experience, men in pain cause most of the deepest problems for girls and women. The pain of men, when shoved down and ignored, ruins so many lives; it's like a nuclear bomb of negative energy, and when it explodes or implodes, it's disastrous to anybody near the blast.

When we are in pain, we are much more likely to hurt others in an attempt to misdirect our attention away from our feelings and to gain a sense of control. It's not an intentional, clear-headed choice. It happens at a deep unconscious level, where we are incapable of making rational decisions at that moment from inside the pain, but it's devastating nonetheless.

> **The more internal control we have,
> the less external control we need.**

Abusive, controlling behavior of any kind or intensity level is always a sign of insecurity, a fear of not being able to deal with a situation. So we believe we have to control the environment, often by force or threats of force. Clearing our pain helps us have true control internally, so we don't need the illusion of control externally.

> **If I can control me,
> I don't need to control you.**

There are two ways to deal with pain. You can either cope with it, which is what most of society is trained to do, or you can clear it.

Coping is like carrying all the sandbags around, using your energy and behavior patterns to try to keep the bags hidden as they get bigger and bigger, heavier and heavier.

Clearing is allowing the sand to ooze out so it doesn't overwhelm you anymore. I believe most men don't do the clearing work because they don't know it's possible, nor do they understand how truly liberating it will be. It may not be easy or quick or comfortable—in fact, it likely won't be—but it's possible, and it's worth it, especially for your daughter's sake.

This same guy, who left his family when Kobe Bryant missed a shot, hasn't dealt with a major anger outburst in years because the deeper underlying pain has been acknowledged and cleared.

I rarely *choose* anger as a response anymore because I've never known it to work well. I can count on one hand the number of times I've been out of control with my negative emotions in the last decade. This work doesn't happen with the quick flip of a switch, but it's doable, for anybody.

For me, there were two deep pains being repressed: the illusion that my mom abandoned me as a child and the underachievement in my baseball career. Looking back now, the sports career disappointment is why I responded so irrationally to Kobe missing his shot. I didn't "win" in my own career, and then my favorite team couldn't win either. Not being able to get a sense of vicarious accomplishment, I threw an impotence tantrum.

It's sad that so many of us men are emotionally connected as much as we are to our sports teams winning. It's totally okay to enjoy the competition, root hard for our teams, and get riled up in the process, but we must do it in a healthy way. When it creates damage to ourselves, our family members, or others, it's clearly not healthy.

> When things we don't control cause us to get angry, we are victims of our suppressed emotions.

Clearing our own emotional pain helps us stay in the space of healthy desire, love, and appreciation, which allows us to express pride and affection with our daughters to the highest degree possible. It allows us to be ourselves. It allows us to be REAL men.

R = Rigid. The masculine energy is naturally rigid in its purest form, meaning inflexible, unyielding, all or nothing, in or out, yes or no. The trait of rigidity is neither good nor bad; its effect depends on what it is protecting with its uncompromising commitment.

We've been conditioned from a young age to be protective of our ego, self-image, and societal ideas of "strength" and "power," mostly defined by other men who are afraid of losing their identities or positions within their male community. The misguided constructs have been passed down from generation to generation.

Instead, we can apply that same level of rigidity to our masculine integrity in its untarnished form. We should be uncompromising in our core values, beliefs, goals, and visions for the sake of protecting friends and family, not using that rigidity *against* friends and family. This kind of healthy rigidity of our masculine essence creates trust from others as well as trust in ourselves because it is consistent, stable, and admirable.

E = Expressive. Expression is the opposite of suppression. Emotions are designed to move through our bodies, not be trapped inside them. The only way to do that is through the safe expression of our thoughts and feelings. Remember—if we don't express them outwardly, where do they go?

Without being let out, the only option is for them to be suppressed inside, with increasing tension, living in our cells until they get released somehow. We have a finite capacity for embodying emotions, just like the saturated towel, so the pressure literally grows and grows and grows until they come out either under control or out of control. But let's be clear—they are coming out at some point because they have to.

The only way our emotions won't be released is if we numb our sensations of them with drugs, alcohol, or other physically and mentally destructive substances, trapping them inside forever. But destroying the biological receptors of our feelings doesn't make them go away; it just kills our ability to feel everything, including joy and pain, in a slow death to our physiology. This is not a better option.

If we hold our emotions in until they become unmanageable, they will usually come out in an aggressive and dangerous manner. But if we allow ourselves to be fully expressive of the full spectrum of emotions, both good and bad, our bodies and minds become clear channels capable of living with intention, emotional control, and a joy-filled presence.

An emotionally expressive man is a safe man.

A = Authentic. This simply means be who you truly are, not who you've been conditioned to pretend to be, not who you think others want you to be. Just you. Your core self. Be transparent. Be truthful. Be open. Be vulnerable. Contrary to what we've been led to believe, vulnerable masculinity is the essence of pure strength, not needing to prove itself to anybody or overcompensate in any way. It's not about creating more masks as we perpetually pretend to be something or someone else, but rather taking all of our false masks off.

Vulnerable masculinity is a superhero of sorts, the unwavering protector of life and goodness, allowing everyone in its presence to be free and happy. We don't have to put forth any effort into our masculinity in its natural state, we just have to stop covering it up and surrender into it. It has healing and protective energy all by itself. It's not *difficult* to be authentic, it's just scary as hell because of our macho programming. But no matter how tough it seems, it's possible, especially if you surround yourself with supportive people who have your best interests at heart.

L = Love. This is the essence of our human experience. In every single moment, we are either operating *with* love or *without* love. When we are with love, we are *giving* love to ourselves and others. When we are without love, we are *seeking* love from ourselves and others. I'm not saying it's necessarily easy, but everything can be boiled down to this very simple dichotomy, and I've found it to be extremely helpful with myself and clients to regain control whenever we're in a "sideways moment."

The idea of masculine love is an interesting one to explore because it's all too rare in our world today, yet so crucially needed. Its powerful effect is quite literally breathtaking because many people have never experienced it. As boys, we're taught that vulnerability is a sign of extreme weakness, so in order to not be taken advantage of, we rarely let it out. But this has such dangerous consequences.

When we deny ourselves our vulnerability, we cut off all of our emotions, including love. In doing so, we are also denying ourselves the sacred human experience, that which gives us a full encounter of life and breath and raw passion. We then deny ourselves the very lifeblood of our masculine needs and desires because vulnerability has now become dangerous to the ego, which is always committed to protecting our self-image.

So, what we have left to carry around is not true masculinity but a warped facade of armor created by the ego, fueled by the fear of loss, and constantly on the lookout for threats. It would be like Superman wearing a costume of Kryptonite.

> Our macho construct of masculinity is, in itself, emasculating.

To watch me perform my TEDx poem about being a R.E.A.L. man, go to www.CoachSeanSmith.com/tedx

What's needed instead is pure fatherly love toward our daughters, of course, but also toward our sons and ourselves. And not just our biological sons but all the boys who are looking up at us wondering what's okay, what's not okay, and what's expected of them in order to stay in good favor with the men they are looking up to and seeking belonging with.

They need to know that vulnerability will not be cause for their dismissal, abandonment, or shaming. But they don't need to hear it with their ears; they need to see it with their eyes. They need to see us men hug each other, feel us be open with our emotions, and hear us say to each other, "*I love you.*"

We, as a community, have to stand up and redefine what being a man really is. We are no longer barbarians on the battlefield, so the archaic rules that served us many generations ago don't serve us anymore. We are family men. We are husbands, fathers, and friends. We have careers, goals, and dreams. We have human thoughts, desires, and feelings. We are here to enjoy this life and help the people around us do the same. It's time to change the paradigm and release the pressure that we've placed on ourselves for far too long.

The old idea that "strong men" don't have fear, don't express emotions, don't show vulnerability, and never act like a "sissy" is all macho BS, and it does more harm than good. Our society, especially women and young girls, is suffering because of it. Let me offer a new paradigm whose time has come...

THE REAL MAN'S MANIFESTO

1. **A REAL MAN** knows the healing power of sacred vulnerability.
   He has the courage to be afraid and conquers anger with humility.

2. **A REAL MAN** is raw, genuine and transparent.
   He knows his masculinity isn't proven, it's inherent.

3. **A REAL MAN** is emotional and lets his feelings flow.
   He's not concerned with losing status if he lets his feelings show.

4. **A REAL MAN** knows his strength will never come from being violent.
   He respects his self control and the wisdom of being silent.

5. **A REAL MAN** faces, embraces and releases his own pain.
   Instead of projecting it, deflecting it or misdirecting it in vain.

6. **A REAL MAN** doesn't need to chase approval from his peers.
   His inner voice of truth is the most important one he hears.

THE REAL MAN'S MANIFESTO
(CONTINUED)

7. **A REAL MAN** leaves everything he's got on the field when he competes.
   He knows that he loses no dignity by admitting his defeats.

8. **A REAL MAN** places value in protecting and providing.
   He spends his time and energy connecting, not dividing.

9. **A REAL MAN** isn't threatened by the differences in others.
   Race, Religion, Sexuality… they are ALL our sisters and our brothers.

10. **A REAL MAN** seeks no pleasure in seeing other people smudged.
    He's committed to a life well lived and loved, more than a life well judged.

11. **A REAL MAN** protects and chases the goals and dreams of his inner boy.
    He understands the pride found in the mirror is the only way to inner joy.

12. **A REAL MAN** can tell the difference between respect and intimidation.
    He knows that his integrity is the most important punctuation.

CHAPTER 14

The Total Truth Letter

IF YOU'RE READY TO TAKE your emotional control to another level, I invite you to write a Total Truth Letter. This is the process I learned in a seminar with Jack Canfield that started my complete transformation many years ago. I've seen countless people release their emotional bondage through this exercise. I swear by it. It is the single most common healing process I do with my clients, especially men.

The process follows the Six Layers of Human Emotion already described. You're going to write a handwritten letter (not typed on the computer), giving an expressive voice to each of these feelings.

Putting pen to paper as opposed to fingers to keyboard gives you a much better connection to your body, emotions, and language. It's a critical part of the exercise. It's important to give this process whatever time and space you need for it because it just might change your life forever, as it has done for me and so many others.

Every emotion gets its own paragraph. Remember, we want to isolate and express each one individually. It's usually best to start with a certain person you have or had a conflict with to better focus the access to your embodied feelings. I always advise clients to start with their parents because we are usually holding onto some measure of anger and resentment toward them.

True to this book's theme, I suggest writing one to your father first. It's almost impossible for any of us to get through childhood without our own daddy issues.

Start by writing everything you are angry about and spend the whole first paragraph on just anger, with NO FILTERS. This process is for you only, so write the letter knowing the other person is never going to read it.

If your anger wants to curse and swear like a maniac, write it down, and get it out. A man's anger usually does. If your anger wants to blame him for everything bad in your life, write it down, and get it out. It's critical that you don't hold back, trying to protect yourself or him by pretending these thoughts and feelings don't exist. You'll never be able to release something until you own its existence. Only then can you let it go. So if it's in your head, put it down on paper so it can be released from your body. This is the ultimate emotional control.

Continue writing until it feels like there's no more anger to express. You'll know you've hit that point when there are no more new thoughts or feelings, as though the anger well has dried up. Allow it to take however long it needs to take. For some, it's only a few minutes for about half a page. For others, it can take twenty minutes or longer and span multiple pages.

Some even write one gigantic run-on sentence that would make any language teacher cringe! All of that is okay. Emotions rarely follow grammatical rules. Regardless of how long or how messy this anger expression is, it's worth it to release and regain control of your emotions, your mind, and your body.

When that's complete, move on to the second paragraph, which is all about pain. The same rules apply to each paragraph—no filters and no protection; write until you've fully expressed the emotion. When there's nothing else to write about pain, write the third paragraph on fear. When that's complete, write the fourth paragraph on regret. After regret, write the fifth paragraph on desire and, finally, the sixth paragraph on love. Six paragraphs of any length, grammatical rules be damned. Six emotions, isolated and expressed. Release.

There's no wrong way to do it. It may not be emotionally or psychologically "easy." It may even get extremely uncomfortable, but it will be worth it, I promise. When you express your anger, clear your pain, and begin releasing all the negative tension, you can be even more present with others and experience greater love and appreciation, especially for your daughter.

Here's a short sample letter to give you some ideas. Yours will almost certainly be much longer, so please don't think this is the model for you to emulate. I'm only giving three sample sentences for each emotion just to give you a sense of the exercise and where your emotions may take you.

Dear Dad,

I'm angry at you for always yelling at me when I tried my best. I'm f***ing pissed that you didn't treat my mom right. I was angry at my ninth birthday party when you showed up late and drunk. Again.

It hurt me when you told your friends from work that I should be a better basketball player and that I don't work hard enough. It hurts every time you "jokingly" tell me I'm your "favorite daughter." It hurt me when you didn't take me fishing that one day when I asked if I could go with you and you said there wasn't room in the boat but you brought three of your sh*thead friends with you instead.

I'm scared that I will turn out to be just like you and treat my wife like you treated Mom. I'm terrified that my sons will feel the same way about me that I feel about you. I'm scared that you won't ever find happiness in life or a marriage.

I regret that we never had the kind of relationship I wanted to have with my only dad. I regret that I didn't make a better effort to communicate with you in my adult years. I regret that my kids never had a chance to be with their grandfather during Christmastime when they were little.

What I really want is for us to be closer. I want to have better communication with you more often. I want to hear more stories about your childhood and early adult years so I can know more about who you were when you and Mom met.

Dad, I love you for trying your best. I love you for being my father when it would have been easier to walk away. I love you for all the lessons you've taught me in my life.

My father died when I was thirty-seven years old. And while none of these sentences above match the actual feelings or incidents I had with him, in these words, I can clearly feel the deep energy of our need for a sacred connection with our dads.

CHAPTER 15

Discipline with Love

ONE OF THE HARDEST PARTS OF PARENTING, I think, is disciplining our children. Of course, there has to be consequences when they break the rules, but *how* you discipline them is critical, especially with girls. In my coaching experiences with adult women, so many of them have emotional pain stemming from their father's discipline tactics. But it's usually not the consequences themselves; it's the disappointment or anger he used to communicate the consequences. That's what cuts the deepest.

Take the higher road, even if it's difficult. Instead of yelling at her in a demeaning way, be emotionally neutral in the discussion about her behavior, while being emotionally loving with your communication about her personally.

As best you can, always keep your conversation focused on the positive, not the negative. When we say things like, "*What's wrong with you?*" or "*What's the matter with you?*" our daughters often take it to mean they themselves are broken, not good enough, or disappointing in our eyes.

But when we change the energy of the questions to "*What's going on?*" or "*How are you feeling?*" or "*Is there anything I can do to help?*" they know we are truly there for them as a protecting and loving dad, even when disciplining the behavior is necessary. And remember, disciplining behavior while loving the "behaver" is immensely powerful and will almost always produce healthy behavioral change that harmful words and seething disappointment never can.

It's definitely not easy if you've never had it modeled this way before, but I promise you it's possible. More importantly, your daughter's heart and self-esteem will remain healthy, even as you dole out punishment for her actions.

For example, let's say your preteen daughter brings home her report card with lower grades than you would like to see. Even though our natural tendency as fixers causes us to want to immediately ask, "*Why did you get that B in Language?*" please don't.

You would likely be amazed at how many times my deep-dive life coaching brought up a version of that exact memory, with that exact phrasing, for my adult women clients. What they often hear is, "*What's wrong with you? Why are you not perfect? You must be perfect to get my approval.*"

A healthier way to handle it is to start with approval by saying, *"I'm so proud of you. Look at all these good grades."* Then, ask how she feels in general, without directing her answer. *"What are your thoughts on your grades?"*

If she says she's happy with them, congratulate her first. And if it's still really important to you to discuss her level of achievement, feel free to do that, but in a caring way that clearly lets her know your approval is not at risk over a letter on a piece of paper. This concept bears repeating—in a way that lets her know your approval is not at risk.

I suggest a question like, *"Are there any grades you would like to improve?"* If she says yes, then the door is open for you to say, *"Excellent, let's talk about some ways you might be able to do that."* Now, you're helping her with something she wants to improve, as a partner and cheerleader, instead of chastising her for not being perfect in your eyes.

But be prepared. If she says no, that there aren't any grades she wants to improve and that she's completely happy with her report card, my advice is to swallow your ego. Her school grades are not a reflection of your performance as a parent, and the damage you can do to her emotions probably isn't worth it.

Of course, there are many gradients in this discussion, and a report card full of Fs and one D is much different than As and one B. But the main point is that unless she gives you an opening to help her fix her grades, the typical you're-not-perfect conversation with Dad likely won't go over well internally for her.

At every step of the way, make sure she knows you are talking about raising her achievement, not her self-value. As boys, we were usually programmed to feel good about ourselves only when our achievement levels were high. With girls, it's generally reversed.

I've learned very clearly that when girls feel good about themselves, their achievement levels increase. And poor performance doesn't have the same deflating effect as it does with boys. So, we must treat them differently than we were treated when it comes to achievement. I believe the way they were naturally programmed is much healthier anyway. It's better to learn from them than to teach them about achievement the way most of us boys were taught.

Let's look at another example: imagine your seventeen-year-old daughter wrecks your expensive car. Remember that although your car is worth a lot of money, her self-esteem is worth more. Ask her if she is okay, physically and emotionally. Allow her to tell you everything or tell you nothing. Be her protector, not her interrogator.

Tell her the car is just a thing, it's replaceable, and that she means more to you than your vehicle. Then ask if she's willing to tell you about the accident. Once she realizes that you're not just there to yell and punish, she's much more likely to open up truthfully.

You have every right, of course, to ask about the accident as a concerned parent and talk about what she can do in the future to stay safe. But notice it's about *her* safety, not your car's. No matter what age, children are much more inclined to be truthful with their parents about their actions when they know their hearts are safe inside the discussion.

My daughter recently backed out of our driveway in a rush to get to school and ran into my car, leaving a long blue scratch on my rear bumper. In my initial reaction, I felt my mind starting to race. I felt the anger starting to build. But then I remembered this chapter and the three paragraphs above I had written months before. Later that day, she apologized, saying she felt terrible. I decided to not even ask about the incident. She had clearly already learned the lesson. So I told her that every time I see the scratch, I'll think of her. She smiled.

In these kinds of situations, learn to love to listen. Listening is a highly valuable skill that most of us haven't learned correctly. One of my favorite concepts is...

Don't listen to fix. Listen to understand.

Most often, when we're listening, we're thinking about what it is we want to say next and looking for the problem to solve, and often what's actually being said to us gets lost.

When you use love to tap into what you feel compelled to communicate, you'll always say the right thing because you'll always be coming from the right place. In coaching, we call this concept the "come from." If your "come from" is clean, your words will always land well. Your energy speaks much louder than the words you use anyway. She will feel it, I promise.

It's important not to just listen with your ears but tune into your daughter with the rest of your awareness too. Pay attention to what you see and what you sense. Notice what she's communicating nonverbally just as much as what she is saying verbally.

A great listening tool is to get on the same level of connection as best you can. Match and mirror her body language and speech patterns. If she's talking quietly and slowly but you respond loudly and fast, she's not going to hear you as well, and it may discourage continued conversation. This is the essence of staying in rapport with another human being, which is critical for trust and influence.

Trust your own intuition too. Listen to your gut. You may just "get a feeling" that something is going on with your little girl. Ask her about it, and then listen. Let her know you're there for her. And then listen. If she's in need of advice, it's best to ask her if she wants it before you offer it without permission.

If she says yes to hearing your advice, ask her first what she'd tell a friend in the same situation. We all have answers inside, but sometimes we just need someone we trust to ask us the questions to help find the answers. If she still seems stuck, of course, give your advice, making sure it's coming from a place of support and care. But when she comes up with her own answers, she will remember them better and stay committed to them longer.

I know some of this might be completely different from what we've experienced ourselves and what we've been taught growing up. But even though it's different and maybe uncomfortable, it's a better way to take care of your daughter's heart. And hopefully, you're very clear that most of this is not about what you say, but rather how you say it. Our children are more susceptible to our energy than we think, especially daughters with their daddies.

CHAPTER 16

Celebrate Her Uniqueness

YOUR DAUGHTER IS ONE OF A KIND. There is no other person exactly like her, even if she is an identical twin. There is something unique about her, and you know it, so share it with her often. Encourage her to be proud of her uniqueness.

Most kids want to fit in with their peer groups to get a sense of belonging. For girls, that desire is usually deeper than for boys because of how much self-worth they derive from being like their friends. So, for girls specifically, being perceived as different can be quite painful unless we can help them see their uniqueness as valuable and important to embrace.

Teach her that the ways she is different will allow her to make a difference in this world. Your daughter's unique talents and abilities were gifted to her to use in this life. They are not meant to be taken for granted. We often discount our unique abilities because to ourselves, they seem normal and maybe even mundane. We don't usually see how the things we take for granted can be valuable to others.

But help her realize that there never has been a human being with her exact combination of gifts, desires, and life experiences, nor will there ever be one again. She is truly one of a kind. Her purpose is not to try to become like anyone else; it's to be the most authentically expressed version of herself, especially her uniqueness.

Each piece of a puzzle has its own shape and its own design. Can you imagine what would happen if all the pieces were the same? Teach her that her beauty is found in the differences that are uniquely her, not in her attempts to be like anybody else.

For example, my wife is a brilliant poet. In 2011, she wrote one poem a day for over 120 days straight, she has rhymed our annual Christmas letter since 2003, and she can come up with amazing rhymes for almost any word. Yet, it's so easy for her to do that she often forgets it is her gift, and she downplays how it makes a difference. But if you ask anyone who's read her poems or received our Christmas update, they've been touched by her talents immensely. It's often what we take for granted in ourselves that is most valued by other people.

Take the time to get to know your daughter's unique talents, and make them a BIG deal. Pay attention to what she does well with ease and enthusiasm. Watch what she gravitates toward when she has free time on her hands. See what distracts her attention and pulls her in quickly, and notice when she spends hours on something and stays excited about it. Profess your pride in her and those things, for they are her glorious gifts to the world.

There are several great quotes you can share with your daughter to remind her of the power of her uniqueness. Some of my favorites are:

"Be yourself. Everyone else is already taken."
—Oscar Wilde

"Always be a first-rate version of yourself and not a second-rate version of someone else."
—Judy Garland

"To be yourself in a world that is constantly trying to make you something else is the greatest accomplishment."
—Ralph Waldo Emerson

"The woman who follows the crowd will usually go no further than the crowd. The woman who walks alone is likely to find herself in places no one has ever been before."
—Albert Einstein

"The more you like yourself, the less you are like anyone else, which makes you unique."
—Walt Disney

> "In a world where you can be anything—be yourself."
> —Etta Turner

> "You are unique, and if that is not fulfilled, then something has been lost."
> —Martha Graham

> "Your uniqueness is the master key that unlocks the hidden treasures of your lifetime."
> —Bryant McGill

When your daughter is young, she will easily be herself. As she grows, she'll learn what society thinks and expects of her, and she may start to change. Some girls change so they don't stand out because they're afraid of being noticed. Others will change so they do stand out. Some will withdraw and hide. Some will rage in anger against the world or the people in it. All of these examples are girls who are further and further away from their true selves, either seeking or afraid of attention for the wrong reasons.

Give deliberate care to these kinds of behavioral changes your daughter is going through, and help her stay true to what makes her unique. In her adolescent years, this may be harder because there's so much emphasis and desire to "fit in." But again, if you've filled her up with how proud you are of her authentically unique self, there's a greater chance she won't change the *essence* of who she is because she will be comfortable with and proud of herself internally.

The key thing to pay attention to is her essence. Of course, children grow and experience significant changes in mind, body, and spirit; it's all a part of healthy growth. But if she seems to be shifting in her energetic nature, there's more cause for concern.

For example, young teenagers tend to be a little sharper and more sarcastic with their tongues as they become more influenced by the media and their peers, which seems to be more and more abrasive these days. They also tend to pull away from the family unit a little more with their time as they develop their own sense of independence, identity, and friendships.

These behavioral shifts are all very normal, and it's best not to place any negative attention or judgments on them. We don't want our little girls to be ashamed of or embarrassed by their growth, especially when their hormones are already raging inside.

The behavioral changes that are more concerning and potential signs of something unhealthy are when they start intending to hurt friends or family members with their language, or they start being vicious with their words toward themselves, or they stop doing things they've always loved to do, or they maybe stop having fun altogether.

This is when it's time to check in with her using your love, pride, and intuition. Ask how she's doing. Ask if she's happy. Ask if she wants to talk. Many times these changes are silent cries for help and attention. The worst thing we can do as fathers is ignore our daughters when they are desperately wanting us to notice.

If she really is going through a rough time and appears to be changing her essence to get approval or attention, this is the time to remind her of her inner beauty, her wonderful uniqueness, and your pride in her, no matter what. Then, explore the behaviors to see what her intentions are. Again, when she knows she has her daddy's unconditional pride, she's more likely to open up truthfully.

All in all, your goal is to help her love all the things that are unique about her spirit and body. Society will teach her to be self-conscious about being different compared to what's popular. Let's teach her to embrace those differences instead. There never has been and there never will be anyone just like her.

CHAPTER 17

Value Her Voice

MOST WOMEN TEND TO SUPPRESS their voices in my coaching experience, which is somewhat tragic because they are much more prone to be emotionally expressive than men are. The reason they suppress their voices is because, at some point in time, they learned that speaking up is wrong or emotionally unsafe. And, you guessed it, this often starts with their fathers.

Teach her that it's okay to have and to express her feelings and opinions. Especially with questions because we were likely taught by our fathers or other authority figures that questions are a sign of stupidity or disrespect. I can't tell you how many of my clients have told me they were harshly taught: "*Don't question authority!*" when we've been discussing their confidence or self-esteem. They then learn to fear or rebel against authority in an unhealthy way or have a negative relationship to questions of any kind.

Of course, there's a line you can teach your daughters not to cross, but don't shut down the whole act of questioning entirely. Otherwise, it can turn into a debilitating belief that she's not allowed to speak up or question anything. Respectfully questioning the rules, or the status quo, or their current life circumstances is immensely helpful for women to be empowered. And it's really the only way we learn as humans.

Women with that unhealthy belief toward speaking up tend to manifest many physical issues with their thyroid glands or throats in general, often related to them shutting down their own voices. Sometimes this turns into autoimmune disorders, which are predominantly found in females and can be devastating to their health.

We men tend to use our voices as weapons, to assault or protect, in an overpowering way, often through yelling to get our points across. Many women do the opposite, preferring to swallow their truth to avoid risking conflict and harm. Or they might learn that the only way to be heard is to yell in a manner that's out of control, which is more of a masculine behavior and generally won't be healthy for her, nor have the effect that she desires.

Many parents shut down questions as a sign of disrespect, but I've learned that fathers from very high discipline environments tend to do it the most, or at least more aggressively. I'm talking about institutions like the military and police and fire departments.

In those environments, people's lives are literally on the line. Questioning authority can lead to severe damage, injuries, and death. They are also highly tough and masculine environments because of the protective nature of the job.

In no way am I indicting the men and women from those institutions or holding any negative judgment toward those duties. In fact, I honor them completely. They put their own lives on the line to protect others, and there's no more honorable choice in my opinion than service at the risk of personal harm. If you have served in that capacity or anything at all close to it, *thank you*.

The point I'm making is that we have to separate our professional identities when it comes to our family. The training you go through is 100 percent necessary for your careers and responsibilities. But when you come home, your little girls are not the enemies or threats that you need to control, nor are they your boardroom adversaries who you need to defeat. They are your daughters.

They are not your soldiers. They are not your officers. They are not your colleagues. They should not be expected to obey orders in the line of duty the way those other people should. Their questions should not be viewed or punished as insubordination. That works, and I would argue that it is totally necessary in certain jobs.

But not at home. You are not her supervisor or commander. You are her dad. I've coached many adult women who tell me, with tears in their eyes, that they wished their dads had parented them like daughters instead of punishing them like soldiers.

I have coached so many women who've been taught to fear *all* questions, both asking and receiving, which robs them of their natural wonder for learning and the safety of exploratory communication. I've also coached women who are now afraid of *all* authority because their fathers ruled over them with such a heavy iron fist.

When you go through high-stress training for high-stress situations where decisions have to be made spur-of-the-moment, the brain learns to react that way everywhere. It thinks all situations are high-stress and that all challenges and conflicts are attacks, so it responds accordingly. It's simply doing its programmed job, and it does it well.

The distinction that will serve both you and your daughter, however, is to remember there are many environments where your job training and behavior are appropriate but not all environments and not with all people. Please give your daughter that benefit.

Sports, the corporate world, and many other professions fit into this discussion as well. But those do not generate the same kind of life-or-death scenarios, so I want to bring them up separately. Again, this problem is not intentional, and I have a lot of compassion for the men who feel emotionally out of control, regardless of the situation. In fact, that usually adds to the problem because we are programmed to fend off any threats of being out of control.

So, if you find yourself in that scenario, where you are struggling to keep your daughters or other family members separate from your career programming, please allow us to support you with the resources found at the back of this book. This is a big problem for our girls, and it's not one that is easy for us to solve on our own as men. Reaching out for help is a sign of extreme wisdom, not weakness, especially when your family's and your emotional health is at stake.

Help her celebrate and value her own voice by showing her that you value it. Teach her to trust her voice and be unafraid to express her thoughts and feelings appropriately, regardless of whether other people agree or disagree. And again, as with so many of these concepts, the best way to instill this in her is to show it with your own actions.

Frequently ask her to share what she thinks. Make it okay for her to disagree with you, and model what it's like to have a healthy, clean conversation between a man and a woman who don't agree with each other. Healthy conflict is not about trying to win or get the other person to change their beliefs. It's about valuing each other's opinions and talking about them without any personal attacks. Never make her wrong about having or expressing her thoughts and opinions, and never make her think that your opinion of her is dependent on her beliefs matching yours.

CHAPTER 18

"Replacement Parents"

I WANT TO ADDRESS A COUPLE of special circumstances where your daughter might be in a replacement situation—adoption, death, and stepfamilies. I know that word "replacement" might seem insensitive, but we have to understand that to a small child, that's how their brains look at it, not consciously or intentionally. But, in reality, the biological parent is not there anymore or never was, and he or she has been replaced with someone else.

Replacement Situation #1—*Stepmoms.*

If your biological daughter has a stepmother who did not give birth to her, it's a significant consideration for you. Girls want to be like their moms, so they often vicariously feel the abandonment when their mother is replaced. Right, wrong, or fair doesn't matter; it's the reality of how a lot of girls feel.

Often times, they will blame, resent, and be angry at you for leaving their mom. Be gentle with those judgments if they are there. You getting angry or defending your new wife or girlfriend won't solve the problem. Listening, loving, and embracing will. Validate her opinions first; then you can address them directly.

Don't try to change her feelings; just listen to them. Don't try to deflect her anger; empower her to let it out. You're big enough and need to be mature enough to absorb it without lashing back at her. It's likely that your daughter has more sadness around the situation and more love for her mom than you do, so your perspectives are nowhere close to the same.

Don't try to get her to adopt your views; just validate hers. The more irrational they seem to you, the more graceful you have to be. Sometimes the nicer the stepmom is, the more the young girl will hate her. Fighting with those feelings isn't going to change them, but helping her express and release them will.

Make it your goal to remain on your daughter's side, not make her choose between her mom and you. You don't have to betray your new partner to support your daughter. If your daughter is angry, you can disagree with what she says, come from a place of love and care, and still validate her as a person.

Replacement Situation #2—*Stepdads*.

Now we're getting a little trickier because you are not her biological father. While all the concepts in this book still apply to your relationship, you have to be sensitive to the fact that you are the replacement. Be as compassionate as you can, even if it's tough.

If she's angry at you, it probably means she has some kind of emotional void or incompletion with her biological dad that is being projected onto you. This is natural, extremely common, and usually unconscious. This might sound counterintuitive, but if she felt whole and complete with her relationship with her father, she wouldn't feel threatened or resentful toward you.

Knowing this, the last thing you want to do is be confrontational with her emotions. No matter how much strife she may have with her biological dad or how much pain he may have caused her, he's still her daddy. She still wants him to love her and to be proud of her. You stepping into the family unit could take away that possibility in her young mind.

In my coaching experience, the more unstable the feelings, the harsher the language. And the more irrational the reasoning, the deeper the pain. You'll never get through that type of deep-rooted emotion quickly, easily, or with force. It can happen, but only with awareness, patience, and compassion.

Let her know openly that you will never replace her dad, nor do you want to. Let her know that your relationship with her is totally separate from his. And never, ever, ever talk badly about him. It's not your place. Even if she is speaking viciously about him, don't join in. If he's out of line in any way, of course, you can support her, but always make it about protecting her and not trashing him. Those are different. You cutting him down is not going to elevate yourself in any kind of healthy way.

Support is what she needs from you the most, not your ability to pile on. There might be times where it's incredibly tempting, and she might even open the door to it, but it's not worth the risk, trust me, nor is it necessary. And please remember, I'm not speaking from morality or academic theory; I'm telling you what women have reported to me about how they take those comments in these situations specifically.

Think about what she might be dealing with that's causing her the deepest pain. It's likely some form of abandonment, whether it be emotional, physical, real, or imagined. So the best replacement you can offer is the opposite of what she's experiencing. In this case, it's stability and unconditional support.

Let her know that you won't leave her. Even when she might not want you to be there, you can show her that you're not going away. That doesn't mean to force yourself into her space when you're not welcome, but you can always be available to her, even if it's just outside the door she closed on you.

Know that she may have made decisions and formed beliefs that aren't positive for you, but that's not anything you can control. Getting angry and using verbal force to wedge your way into her life isn't the way to change those decisions. Being open, honest, caring, compassionate, and stable is the way.

And this should go without saying, but I'm going to say it because it's so important. Do not make her choose between her biological father and you in any way whatsoever. You cannot be him, you cannot replace him, and you cannot pretend she came from your genes when she did not. If she makes that choice on her own, great. But don't try to force the choice. And contrary to what many stepdads think, separating yourself from that biological role will actually give you better access to her heart and cause her to trust you more.

I also urge you to not force your philosophies on discipline onto her or her mother. The traditional *"My way or the highway"* and *"I know how to enforce the rules that her father never did"* aren't going to be helpful from *her* perspective. The road you're traveling is already challenging enough and fraught with anxiety, pain, or stress. Be gentle. Be willing to yield when appropriate instead of always trying to take over. And what you'll likely find is that both she and her mom will be more welcoming to any of your unique styles and traits that differ from what they were used to with him.

This all varies by age and individual circumstances, of course, so use your best judgment and intuition. Make the absolute best of the situation. You won't be able to take his place, but you have a special role with her that brings its own uniqueness.

You absolutely can create an amazing connection and relationship with her, no matter how much pain she might be in. I've heard plenty of stories of women who were 100 percent against their stepfather, but they were eventually won over through kindness and consideration, not force. The more you fully embrace and authentically express your place in her life and the more you take care of her emotions toward her biological father, the more value you can add to her life and vice versa.

Replacement Situation #3—*Deceased Moms.*

Whether you've gotten into a new relationship or not, daughters dealing with the death of their mother are managing a highly traumatic experience. Please don't force her to grieve the same way you are grieving, whether that's healthy or not.

Her relationship with her mom is completely different than your relationship with her mom. So the feelings of loss and sadness are not going to be handled the same way. The best thing you can do is listen to her heart openly and show her yours.

For example, instead of offering phrases like "*We have to move on*" or "*She's in a better place*" or anything else that might be helping you manage your own grief, allow your daughter's experience to be whatever it is. Ask open questions like "*How are you feeling, sweetheart?*" or "*Will you share your thoughts with me?*" or "*If your heart could speak right now, what would it say?*"

Be prepared for and embrace whatever she says. What often comes out when a girl or woman is invited to express her grief is very intense. Because you may not have been exposed or encouraged to share your heart openly, it might get extremely uncomfortable. You might feel the urge to manage the perceived messiness of fully embodied feminine emotion. This is a most critical time for both of you.

Embrace the connection of deep human pain without trying to fix it or stop it or control it. What happens for a father and daughter inside such raw vulnerability is sacred and priceless. The less comfortable it is, the more necessary it is—for both of you.

Times of deep grief are difficult and potentially very dangerous when two people aren't managing their emotions in a clean way. But if you come together and connect inside the very sadness that's causing the pain, it can be immensely healing and bring you closer than ever before.

One of the most common complaints of women who have experienced the early death of their mothers is that their fathers seemed to never speak of her anymore. While that's usually because the father wasn't comfortable with his own emotions and ability to grieve, it sends a message to the daughter that her dear mom has been forgotten or dismissed and even the mention of her name is now taboo.

Even though it's uncomfortable and will no doubt bring sadness, have open conversations about her mom in an honorable, loving space. Avoidance will never heal the wounds, and it can, in fact, drive a wedge between the two of you, whether it's something she's conscious of or not. Remember, emotions buried alive never die, especially grief.

Replacement Situation #4—*Adopted Daughters.*

All of the conversations throughout this book apply to adopted girls as well. But what's unique about adoption compared to the three situations above is that the child no longer has either of her biological parents.

Adopted children, at some point, have to deal with their feelings of abandonment and/or betrayal, no matter how healthy or unhealthy their biological family was. And regardless of how you try to look at it in a positive way, from her perspective, the fact is that her parents gave her up for adoption. Because adoption is often perceived by the child as an intentional act of abandonment, many girls carry that pain around their entire lives, and it ends up affecting them in so many ways, both known and unknown to them.

What you have to remember as her dad is that she "lost" her entire biological unit from her viewpoint. It might seem strange to use the word "entire" when talking about only two people. But when you realize all the different emotional roles that parents play in a child's life, it's much bigger than just the two human bodies who are no longer there.

Even if she was adopted at birth, there's still an intuitive knowing that the body which nested, nurtured, and gave birth to her is missing. Some girls deal with that better than others, but there's always some level of physical trauma nonetheless. For some, it's minor. For others, it's completely devastating.

The wound might be so deep and pervasive that she might not even be aware of how much control over her it has. She could feel an all-encompassing sense of sadness or unworthiness that goes well beyond her conscious capacity to understand it. So, once again, one of the best things you can do is meet her with compassion.

I won't pretend to be an academic expert on adoption or any of these replacement situations, for that matter. I didn't learn any of this from textbooks or classrooms. But my coaching experience has taught me that adopted girls generally have a deep-rooted fear of abandonment, a desperate craving for stability, and a strong belief they are unlovable, whether it's conscious or not.

That last one is a belief that I urge you to attack with ferocious advocacy. Of course, treat her adoption and feelings with the same openness and validation as I'm preaching throughout this book, and never speak badly about her biological family. But specifically make her know that you chose her. You *chose* her. You chose *her*. Willingly. Trust me, that matters a lot.

The deepest pain for most adopted girls is that their biological parents *intentionally* gave them up. So meet that belief with the same concept of intentionality. Not only did you intentionally choose her once, you continue to choose her over and over and over again because of how beautiful, special, and valuable she is.

The other deep wound adopted girls often carry is the pain of not belonging, especially if there are significant physical differences, such as skin color or other contrasting features compared to her adopted family members. Remember that girls are judged more on their physical features than boys are, so anything negative or different related to their bodies can be especially difficult for them to deal with.

Lean heavily on her uniqueness being even more valuable when she's adopted. It's best that she doesn't try to become like the rest of the bunch, but rather adds her own distinct brilliance and beauty to the family puzzle. I suggest learning about her biological culture if it differs from yours so you can celebrate her heritage with dignity instead of her believing she has to throw away who she was and where she came from in order to fit in.

As she grows, you can help her reframe her adoption as positively as possible by offering her a different belief than "*I'm unlovable.*" One of my clients found peace around her adoption by deciding that her biological mother loved her so much that she chose to give her to a family that had the love and stability she deserved in this world, rather than keeping her trapped in her mother's painful circumstances.

The more grace and compassion you show her, the easier it will be for her to fully embrace and trust you as her father and herself as a beautiful, unique part of the family.

CHAPTER 19

Be Her Biggest Fan

ONE OF THE BEST WAYS TO FILL her up with your pride in her is to be her biggest fan, no matter what. Whatever she's into, celebrate it. You may not love dance recitals, music performances, soccer, or anything else unfamiliar to you, but if she's exercising her talents in these arenas, cheer for her like you would your favorite football team. Or if you prefer theater and art but your daughter is into sports, do your best to attend her events and appreciate her efforts like you would an outstanding theatrical performance.

I'm not saying to tell her she's the best if she's not, but it's important to be her biggest fan, regardless of her talent level. Cheer for her loudly so she knows someone's rooting for her. She needs to know, as life goes on, that she's got you in her cheering section, no matter what, and that your support is not conditional upon her good performance.

You can take it a step further by talking with your daughter about her interests. Find out exactly what she loves about whatever she loves. Maybe even try taking up one or more of her passions, if they're not already yours, to get an inside perspective and understanding of what's really going on when she's participating in "her thing." Even if you don't deeply enjoy the activity, you'll have a common, shared experience to discuss for hours on end.

Your involvement in her interests can do wonders for your daughter's self-worth because it signifies to her that she's important. It lets her know you like her, not just love her because she's your daughter. You will encourage her love, acceptance, and appreciation of herself, which keeps her from needing to go outside of herself to find them.

As your daughter's cheerleader, you can also help curb comparisons. It's natural for us as humans to compare ourselves to others. However, when we have someone rooting for us and cheering us on, it helps us focus on ourselves and improve our own performance instead of constantly seeking approval from all the outside influences.

If you notice your daughter comparing herself to others, encourage her to only compare her present situation with her past. For example, if your daughter runs track or swims or does any sport where they are timed for their performance, she should look at her progress—did she do better than last time? If not, focus on her effort and find some level of progress in it. There's always something you can celebrate if you look hard enough for it. She's worth it.

If your daughter participates in what I call a "judgment sport"—such as gymnastics, figure skating, dancing, cheerleading, etc.—where one or more judges will determine the value of her performance, please stay in her ear closely and constantly. These sports reinforce the pattern of her giving her best effort, then waiting for somebody else to decide how valuable her performance was, based on their own subjective opinions.

For example, you can break down certain elements of the performance and help her see the improvement. Or ask if she was prepared and gave it all she had. At the end of the day, that's the only thing she can control, so it's the only thing she should judge herself on. If she can walk away focusing only on what she controls, she will always be more emotionally stable and feel better about herself.

No matter what, cheer. If she falls down, cheer that she got back up. If she wins first place, cheer. If she finishes last, cheer. Cheer her effort, cheer her attitude, and cheer her unconditionally because she's your little girl trying her best.

Let her also hear you share and brag with others about how proud you are of her efforts and accomplishments. It's one thing for her to hear your praise directly, but it fills a different place in her heart when she hears you sing her praises to other people. Even if she seems uncomfortable with too much of it, that's better than her not knowing how much you support her. She's listening, so keep rooting unconditionally for her.

CHAPTER 20

Don't Be a Disappointed Dad

DISAPPOINTMENT IS THE OPPOSITE OF PRIDE. It's a poisonous word that will never make anybody feel better about themselves. Did your parents ever say they were disappointed in you? If so, how did you feel? Think about the wording—disappointed IN you. Children almost always will internalize that word to the point that it poisons their self-esteem.

There aren't many phrases more painful to a child. They tend to receive it as if it means they have no value. The word "disappointed" itself can create a poor self-image or negative belief that literally lives with them for the rest of their lives. I've seen it many times.

So don't ever be a "disappointed" dad. I put it in quotes because I suggest you never use the word at all. It's not necessary; there are always other ways to describe your feelings, especially when you're focused on behaviors instead of who she is as a person.

You can be "upset" that the judge didn't see the same routine you saw, or "bummed" that her best efforts didn't produce a win as she hoped, or "concerned" about her performance in school. None of those words have the same venom that disappointment does. I've literally seen grown women start crying in an instant when thinking about the disappointment their fathers expressed toward them.

But more than the word itself, make sure you don't *show* disappointment with your body language, energy, tone of voice, loud sighs, and eye rolls. A lot of times, those are even worse. Always remember your "come from."

There are a couple of ways of making sure you don't throw disappointment onto your daughter. The first and best way is by clearing your own pain, as described previously, so there's no internal disappointment for you to project outwardly onto her.

Even if you haven't achieved all your dreams (I've never met anyone who has), don't allow your own disappointment from your past to poison your daughter's joy. Find a way to forgive and be proud of yourself, which shows her how she can forgive and be proud of herself as well, no matter what.

The second way is to take 100 percent responsibility whenever possible. If your daughter does something that irritates you, how can you take responsibility for it? Of course, the actions were hers, but what could you have done differently leading up to it? This isn't meant to absolve her of her responsibility, but rather to soften the way you respond and give yourself more emotional control. Is there something you could have taught her that would have eliminated or changed the action that "caused" the disappointment in you?

That word is in quotes because disappointment is *your* judgment, and you choose your reaction. Knowing that, is there something you could have done differently in the past, and therefore, can do differently in the future, to change what happened and avoid *your* experience and judgment of disappointment in her accomplishments?

Or, as in my case with my baseball career, maybe there is something from your past you are holding on to with shame or disappointment that you need to release—not just for your own emotional well-being but also so you don't have access to the disappointment to project onto your daughter or other people.

Again, this isn't an attempt to take ownership of the actions away from her, just a way to curb your potentially negative reaction by adding an awareness of responsibility on your end too. Plus, it gives you something to adjust in the present moment or near future that helps remove or diminish the powerless feelings that often drive shame and disappointment. You can and should still speak with her about the actions, just without the excessive negative emotions.

When we avoid responsibility, we don't have anything that can change in the future, so the irritation gets triggered easier because, on top of the disappointment, we also perceive ourselves to be out of control. But when we identify an ingredient that can change, we have much more control of our emotions in that particular context. That's the main purpose of taking responsibility.

I don't expect you to be the perfect parent by any means. I know I will never be. All we can do is try our best, obviously. But I hope all of this awareness about what your daughter really needs from you will help both of you live with more peace and joy in your lives. Life is way too short to live any other way.

CHAPTER 21

Become the Man You Want Her to Marry

THIS CHAPTER TITLE COULD HAVE BEEN the entire book! When I first wrote those words, I cried. I thought about the happiness I want for my daughter, the joy she deserves in life, and the perfect spouse for her—one who will need to pass *through me* first!

Before we go any further, this chapter title and frame of reference is from my personal experience with my own daughter, therefore it is written from the heterosexual perspective for both she and I. I want to honor and relay to you the way this realization came to me.

In no way am I intending to exclude, dismiss or offend any gender identity or sexual orientation. The purpose of this chapter is for you to find the leverage of a meaningful profile that you can personally become for the sake of your daughter's happiness. The essence of this lesson applies across all relationships and orientations, both yours and hers.

Now, if you're anything like me, it will be *very hard* for anybody to live up to the enormously high standards you've set for your daughter's life partner, right? It's okay to have those high standards, but the best way to make her believe that that person actually exists is to *show her*.

One of the biggest problems young women have in relationships is not believing that it's possible to find a partner who will treat them right, respect them, love them, cherish them, honor them, and be loyal to them. Many times, it's because they never saw it in real life. So instead, they settle for what's probable instead of believing in what's possible. Show her what's possible in a relationship, what's possible in a great spouse, and what she deserves. She's watching, I promise.

I have a certain night burned into my memory that I am sure will never be forgotten. I stood in the kitchen as my wife came home. Both my son and daughter sat on the living room couch in the dark, watching TV. All the lights in the house were off, so I could only see their faces by the light of the television screen.

As my wife and I hugged in the kitchen, I opened my eyes over her shoulder to see my children. My four-year-old son stared intensely straight ahead at the cartoon, but my seven-year-old daughter was fixated on us. Because it was so dark, she couldn't see our facial features very well, so I imagine she didn't realize I was watching her as she was watching us.

For what seemed like minutes but was probably just a precious few seconds, I noticed her soaking it all in. In that moment, she was learning from our example what a marriage is supposed to look like, what love is supposed to feel like, and what two people do when they deeply care for each other.

Now, I'm not saying that all marriages should look and feel like mine. I share this story because of the intensity of my realization in that moment that our children are always, always, always watching and learning from us. Please take that seriously, and show them what you want them to believe is possible in life and in love.

You will be your daughter's first innocent crush, the model for what she hopes to have in her own life. You can't tell her she deserves one thing, yet show her another. If you hold this chapter title as the guiding principle that governs all your choices, you'd be amazed at how much easier it is to control your behaviors, make wise choices, and create joy in your life. Remember…

> Our children aren't listening to the lectures, they are watching the show.

We have to display what we want them to learn and how we want them to live. Model it for them; don't mention it to them. Your daughter is always watching you and deciding what's possible in her own life.

There's a simple exercise to help you with this. It's only two steps:
1. *Write down all the characteristics you want her future spouse to have.*
2. *Become those characteristics.*

When little girls don't see sensitivity in their fathers or peace in their parent's relationships, how can they model it or attract it in their own lives? They don't know it's even possible. While your daughter needs to see you as strong so she feels confident you will protect her, she also needs to see you being sensitive if you want her to marry someone who will be sensitive toward her.

She needs to see you take care of the women in your life if she is going to attract someone who takes care of her heart. She needs to see you create and protect happiness if she is going to be with someone who does that for and with her.

Of course, your relationship with her mother or your other partners if you're no longer with her mother will not always be perfect, but set the example according to what you want her to see. Show her how you get through rocky times together; demonstrate that you can work together and find peace in your relationship in all circumstances. She needs to see it in order to believe it.

If you happen to be divorced or never married her mother, you still have influence. Even if you only see your daughter on weekends and Wednesday nights or just once a month, she's learning.

It's not about the amount of time she's watching, it's about what she sees when she is.

The more open you are in discussing your relationship, especially with her mother, the better. Be honest about the challenges you've had or the mistakes you've made, and teach her how to avoid them as best she can. Too often, relationships are taboo subjects, which leaves it up to our daughters to figure them out on their own in the trenches.

Be proactive. Ask her what she wants and remind her what she deserves. Have her write her own list of what she wants in a relationship partner, and discuss the list openly with her. If you really want some help becoming the person on that list, promise her that you will. There's nothing like the leverage found in our daughters when we make a sacred vow to them.

No matter what relationship circumstance you're in and what mistakes you've made in the past, it's never too late to become the spouse you want her to marry. If you don't feel you're capable, get professional support. Her future happiness just might be on the line.

CHAPTER 22

Protect Her Dreams With Everything You've Got

WHEN SHE'S YOUNG, YOU ARE the keeper of your daughter's dreams. She may see herself as the princess and you as the handsome prince who comes to make her dreams come true to live happily ever after. Let her live in that fairytale until she outgrows it on her own.

That's what you want for her, anyway, to live happily ever after, right? As a child, her happily ever after is knowing that she's safe, feeling like she belongs, and having the opportunity to explore and enjoy her own experiences and then return to her routine and her home, where she feels loved and protected.

Provide that for her. Play with her to demonstrate that her little girl dreams are important. Listen to her talk, and see what lights her up, what gets her excited. Many of my clients grew up being told that: *"Children should be seen and not heard."* Absolutely not. The wisdom that comes from their mouths as they grow up is incredible if we take time to listen and celebrate it. And it lets her know that her mind is valuable.

Most dreams die too young. If your daughter dreams of being a ballerina, let her take lessons and chase those dreams until she doesn't love it anymore. You can teach her to complete her commitment, whether it be a class, or a season, or a contract, and then let it go.

Listen and learn what she'd like to explore next, and encourage it. Be open to opportunities that don't even appear on your radar. We were never little girls, so we don't know what it's like to chase little girl dreams and get full support from Dad.

> Unchased dreams of the heart become nightmares of the soul.

As boys, we were usually taught that changing our goals and dreams is quitting and quitting is weakness. *"Quitters never win, and winners never quit."* So many of us stayed focused on activities long after we stopped loving them. For girls, it's even more critical to stay connected and committed to their heart's dreams and to love what they're doing as long as possible.

Way too many women are carrying around guilt and resentment for never fully chasing their dreams in both childhood and adulthood. They often think it's not okay to commit to their heart's desires or even have desires at all, which can present much greater emotional problems in life beyond just their goal setting.

Sometimes the feeling gets so exaggerated that they believe they can't have the relationships they want, the success they want, or even true love because they learned dreams are "childish" and they need to grow up to become an adult. Instead, teach her that not only is it okay to chase those dreams, but you will be right by her side the whole time, fighting with everything you've got for everything she wants.

This is controversial for a lot of men, but I believe you should teach your daughter that quitting is okay. There's a commonly held belief that quitting is bad, wrong, or weak. But, in reality, it depends on what you're quitting and why.

Let your little girl know that quitting a certain thing is not the same as giving up entirely. If she gives up on her goals and dreams, that should trigger a response from you because it shows she's either not trying or she's stuck and needs help.

But if she quits something that no longer makes her happy and moves on to something else that does, it is important for you to acknowledge her decision and support what she's going after instead. Remember, you're supporting her happiness, not just the activities.

Think about her quitting from a relationship standpoint. If she was in an unhappy, unfulfilling, or abusive relationship, you wouldn't want her to just "stick it out" would you? Many of my clients have stayed in terrible relationships or unhappy jobs mainly because they were taught that quitting is never an option and they didn't want to be viewed as weak. We need to teach them the ability to discern between healthily quitting things that no longer serve them and unhealthily giving up when minor challenges arise.

Giving up is passive, meaning there's no forward action associated with it. In contrast, quitting and redirecting their commitment is active. We're just switching lanes, not jumping out of the car. We've identified that something isn't working to make us happy anymore and are intentionally making a change because we don't like where that other road was heading. Contrary to popular teaching, successful people are quitting constantly and doing it consciously.

Think of it this way—if you have a goal to get to a certain destination on a road trip but a twenty-car pileup shuts down the freeway you're supposed to travel on, would it be quitting to take a detour? Of course not. It actually shows more commitment to the ultimate goal when you're willing to be flexible as new information shows up.

If the ultimate goal of your daughter's life is joy and happiness, then her decision to make adjustments and take appropriate detours along the way is a sign of wisdom, not weakness. As boys, too often we let our egos talk us out of quitting. Let's not impart the programming onto our girls that quitting equals weakness; it's not a natural belief. Nor is it true.

If you have resentment around your own unchased dreams, share those. Show her your heart, and invite her into some of those activities if possible. Play catch with her, take her to the golf course, play drums for her, or whatever your younger dreams were. Even if she doesn't love the activities themselves, you'd be surprised at how interested she might be when she sees your love wrapped around them.

Invite her to share other things you might love, too, even if they're not typical "girl activities" according to society's norms. Take her fishing, climb trees with her, and show her how to skip rocks. When you take the time to share some of your favorite things, it signifies that she's important because you're sharing something important to you.

As she grows, continue to engage her in conversation about what makes her happy. What does she want to achieve in her life? When she grows old, what does she want to look back and be remembered for? How does she want to make a difference? Have her describe her dreams in as much detail as she can muster, then talk about ways to make them come true. Never let that dream switch be turned off just because she grows older and her dreams change.

Teach her how to set goals and create action plans for those goals. Show her by doing it yourself with your own goals. And then set goals together for the two of you.

The goals themselves matter less than her learning the process of turning her desires into reality. If that's something you struggle with or don't know how to teach her, let me offer some guidance from what I've learned along my personal development journey. Many of us either were never taught or have forgotten how to set and achieve goals.

The best way to choose a goal is to follow your passion. What lights you up when you think about it? What do you dream about doing or achieving? What are you so passionate about that you lose track of time or forget to eat when you're doing it? Listen to the passion inside your heart—it's there for a reason. I believe the main reason the passion exists is for you to take action toward the target that excites you the most.

At the beginning of the goal-setting phase, it's crucial that you don't allow your mind to get caught up in the "how" it's going to happen or the likelihood of it happening. Let your heart dream, and put it down on paper.

It's okay if you end up changing your mind once you're in motion and receive valuable feedback, but never shut yourself down before you even get started. The intellectual ego will often do that because it's afraid of failure and embarrassment. The heart doesn't care about that. Our hearts are more afraid of living in regret of never trying.

Once the passionate goal is identified, it's time to start the strategy phase. Gather any information that's necessary, research best practices, learn techniques, hire coaches, find mentors, or join clubs or organizations—anything that will help you prepare a game plan for achieving this goal.

Once you have a game plan, your new goal is now working on the game plan, not necessarily achieving the actual target. *This* is the most important piece of achievement. You no longer set your sights on the achievement of the goal because the unconscious mind wants an immediate, measurable, tangible path to follow and the achievement of this goal is somewhere out in the future. Whether it's a short-term goal that can be achieved over the next few weeks or a long-term goal that will take several years, it's not going to be something you can achieve immediately.

However, following your game plan is absolutely something you can achieve right away. This not only gives your unconscious mind a tangible, measurable, immediate target, but it also gives you a sense of progress and completion every single time you take a step toward your goal.

The mind craves the sense of accomplishment, and the only way to give yourself that feeling constantly is to focus more on the *process* than the goal itself. Trust me, this is even more critical for girls, who really want to enjoy the journey toward their goals way more than we were probably programmed or allowed to do when we were young boys.

Of course, you'll want to think about the long-term goal to provide motivation and inspiration, but you want to focus and judge yourself on following the plan. You also want to track your progress along the game plan so you can get valuable feedback as to whether you are on pace or not, especially if the goal has a deadline attached to it. If you notice that you are not on pace, you must make adjustments to get yourself back on pace or on track, but don't consider this a failure.

One of the most glaring distinctions between highly successful people and those who don't achieve their goals is the internalization of "failure." When you take the steps toward your goal and you're not getting the results you want, it doesn't mean you are failing. And more importantly, it doesn't mean *you* are a failure. Making those kinds of judgments is the quickest way to guarantee you won't succeed at hitting your goal, or if you do succeed, it will only make you more miserable.

Remember the separation between person and performer? This is how we apply that delineation in the goal-setting process. The outcomes along the journey toward our goals are *feedback*, not failure. When you make that distinction internally, it allows you to keep moving forward without all the emotional turmoil that most people experience when they're not getting the expected results right away. This will be one of the most valuable lessons you can teach your daughter regarding the pursuit of success. Without this lesson, the people who succeed but who lose themselves, their integrity, or their joy in the process, have truly failed.

As you are working on your game plan, it's important to track the actions and outcomes you want to measure. Whether that means a checklist on a digital app or a spreadsheet with pencil and paper, give yourself the visual sense of progress and measurability. If the progress looks to be on track, keep working the plan. If it looks to be offtrack, make a change in the plan. It's that simple. As long as you don't take the feedback personally, there's no reason anybody can't achieve a realistic goal with this mentality.

A great way to keep you motivated along the journey is to celebrate yourself. But not just when things go well; make sure to acknowledge your effort and determination during the times of adversity that are bound to happen while working toward any worthwhile goal. The celebration doesn't have to be extravagant, it could be an enjoyable reward like a movie or massage or even just a simple verbal acknowledgment. But we all like to receive "attaboys" when we are putting in the effort, so make sure to give them to yourself.

Another really important piece of goal setting is accountability.

We are not wired to get the most out of ourselves on our own. Our brains are actually more driven by the desire for comfort and protection than the desire for achievement when left to their own devices.

Offer to be your daughter's accountability partner or request that she be yours, so you can help each other stay connected and committed to the process. I've never seen anybody succeed at achieving their biggest goals and dreams on their own, but most people are trying to do it that way, especially us "macho" men who can do everything by ourselves because we're strong! We have to let that programming go and make sure it doesn't get transferred to our daughters.

Whether you end up hitting the goal or not, make sure to embrace the lessons you learned along the way. I suggest having a discussion with somebody and writing thoughts down to help solidify the learning. As long as you learned the lessons of a journey, you cannot fail. In fact, I believe the main purpose of pursuing your goals is not the achievement of the goals, but rather the lessons to be learned along the way that will make you a better person and more prepared for the next challenge.

Speaking of the next challenge, once you embrace the lessons, it's time to set the next target and repeat the process all over again. Having a supportive partner is always going to help you maximize your lessons and your achievements, especially during challenges. Even if you're working on different goals, accountability can benefit both of you and strengthen your bond further.

If you have any questions or want more support with your goal-setting efforts, please reach out to us, and we'll be happy to help. You'll find contact information in the back of this book.

As you move from goal to goal, remember that dreams change for most of us as we mature. Your little girl may want to be a princess when she's three, an actress when she's six, own a pony when she's ten, and be a professional soccer player when she's twelve, an architect when she's thirteen, a scientist when she's fourteen, a singer when she's sixteen, a YouTuber later when she's still sixteen, and a teacher when she's twenty. Embrace every second of it, buckle up, and enjoy the ride!

The one dream that hopefully doesn't ever change is her desire to live happily ever after. It won't always be available, of course; life isn't easy, nor do we succeed all of the time. But happiness can always be her compass, her highest commitment, and chosen in any situation, especially when it's found inside herself with love and appreciation.

Happily. Ever. After. Protect that one with everything you've got, Dad. She's counting on it.

CHAPTER 23

She Will Always Need You

DON'T EVER THINK OTHERWISE.

No matter what is happening in her life, good or bad, tough or easy, she needs her dad. *How* she needs you will change as she grows, but *that* she needs you never will.

She needs to know you got her. She needs to know you love her. She needs to know you will always be with her and never against her. She needs to know you will fight to protect her heart against any and all threats or enemies.

She needs to know you like her. She needs to know you want to spend quality time with her. She needs to know you trust her. She needs to know you are real with her. She needs to know you have pain and fears and doubts and dreams. She needs to know you are safe.

She doesn't need to know that you're perfect. But, above all, she needs to know you're proud.

In my experience as a coach, what I have found is that most of us suffer from the belief that we're "not good enough" in one area or another. This feeling often sabotages us from reaching our goals and expanding beyond our comfort zones. What I would love is to help every single person realize that we *are* good enough simply because we *are*. Because we exist and have experienced a human journey, we have value and deserve all the success we desire.

If every dad helped his daughter(s) to believe this, the world would be a much brighter place. So many women currently hide their light and refuse to let their brilliance shine because of this belief. But if we can help our daughters change this trend, there would be a powerful glow and healing across the globe. And when we, as men, become more vulnerable and authentic, that glow will be protected with true strength and honor.

How can you do this? Simply by implementing what I've shared in this book. By telling your daughter how *proud* you are of her, how much you *love* her, and how much you *like* her, and by showing her how much you *respect* her and *appreciate* her, by *cheering* her on and *advocating* for her (no matter what), and by *embracing* her uniqueness and *connecting* with her from your heart.

When you believe your daughter is good enough just the way she is and you care enough to show her, you can help her build that belief too. Your pride in her will encourage her to develop beyond her doubts, to risk in order to receive the rewards, and to face her fears. She will feel a greater sense of freedom knowing you will always be there for her, beaming with pride.

Your daughter is yours for life, and you are hers. Let that life be filled with love and pride. Pour it on every day. Thick. Be relentless with it. Embrace her, encourage her, and envision greatness for her.

The majority of her life will be after she leaves the safety of your home. What will you plant in her heart that she will always take with her on her life's journey? That's what matters most. Speak constant, limitless, unconditional love and pride into her head and heart so often and so fervently that your voice will never be turned off inside her mind.

Thank You, Dad

I AM HONORED TO HAVE SPENT this time with you, sharing what I've learned on my journey so that you and your baby girl can benefit in some precious way. I hope it landed with the spirit and intention in which I wrote it.

Fathering ain't easy. It's a very tall and sometimes extremely difficult task. I honor you for being the kind of man who cares enough to pick up a book like this and read it to the end. We need more of you in this world, protecting and empowering our girls and women.

We need men like you who are willing to do the inner work, to look in the mirror and feel the discomfort but lean in anyway because our families are worth it. I've also found it extremely helpful when times get tough to connect with and even have a chat with my little boy inside. If you're like me, you made some promises to him in your younger years about what you want, what you won't tolerate, and what you are willing to fight for in this lifetime. Keep those promises to him.

On behalf of your beautiful daughter, no matter how old she is, I thank you. If she wasn't worth the world to you, you would have stopped reading this book a long time ago. Go tell her that. She probably needs to hear it right now.

And from one dad to another, one man to another, thank you for all of the time you've spent in the trenches, doing what you do for those you love most. Thank you for your effort. Thank you for your courage. Thank you for your bravery.

Thank you for all the days and nights you've spent hustling and fighting and protecting and trying your best. Thank you for holding up the weight of the world so your family wouldn't have to. Thank you for the time you've put in when nobody was watching, when nobody noticed, that nobody acknowledged.

I see you. I feel you. I love you.

I am full of emotion and visible tears as I finish these final words. This work is immensely important for our girls, for ourselves, for our planet. Just as you are.

I'm proud of you, Dad.

Love, Sean

Tips from Our Community

I WANT TO SHARE SOME IDEAS from our community. I asked three questions:

1. Fathers, what positive advice do you have for other dads about what's important to teach our daughters?

2. Ladies, what are you thankful that your father taught you?

3. Ladies, what do you wish your father would have taught you?

"Teach Your Daughter…"
Tips shared by fathers

- Enroll her in karate classes as soon as possible. It greatly builds self-confidence so she is able to make decisions without being unduly influenced by her peers. And as she gets older, she can protect herself against date rape, abuse, or other dangerous situations.

- Teach her everything historically taught to a son: carpentry, plumbing, auto mechanics, yard care, sports, finances, investing, etc. It will help her self-confidence, save her a lot of money by doing things herself, and develop a "teamwork" thought process advantageous in both business and personal relationships.

- Teach her how to respect other people. Simple things like never be late to meetings, don't interrupt when others are speaking, etc.

- Teach her to call her parents and grandparents frequently and visit or support them when possible.

- Teach her to look for the reasons people are angry, like underlying pain and fear. It will help her be compassionate and avoid taking other people's actions personally.

- Teach her to do more listening than talking when engaging with others.

- Teach her to be kind.

- Teach her to not let anyone tell her what she can or can't do in this life.

- Teach her that she determines her worth, nobody else.

- Teach her that girlfriends and boyfriends will come and go, but families are forever.

- Teach her to avoid getting mixed up in other people's drama.

- Teach her that she is absolutely beautiful—just as she is.

- Teach her to treat others with respect.

- Teach her that life is short, so forgive other people. The only person you hurt when you don't forgive others is yourself.

- Teach her to love others unconditionally and tell them often how much you love them. Do that with yourself too.

- TALK to your daughter. Talk about anything. Let her talk about anything. It doesn't matter what she says, just be there for the conversation. When your daughter knows you're always there for her and knows she can talk to you about anything, when she has something hard, or scary, or earth-shifting to talk about, she will be more likely to come to you—and THAT can save her life.

- Rather than protecting your daughter from the world, give her your strength, and help her develop her own.

- Teach her to be honest, learn more than one skill, and never let a boy or a man treat her poorly because she always deserves to be treated like a queen. Do this by letting her see how you treat her mom.

- Teach her to never be a thief of someone's time. If you are on the time clock, you are working! Do the job right the first time, and do a job that you will be proud of.

- Teach her to learn through reading books and talking to others.

- Teach her that her honesty and integrity make her respectable.

- Teach her to treat the people who serve her with respect and generosity.

- Teach her to be comfortable with difficult conversations by listening to whatever she has to say. Go to bat for her when it comes to her passions and goals.

- Teach your daughter how important she is by having a monthly date day, just the two of you. Do whatever she wants to do, and listen to her. Show her how a man should treat a woman on a date.

- Teach your daughter to be consistent, to say what she means and mean what she says.

- Teach your daughter respect by talking to her like she's an adult and by answering her questions directly.

- Teach your daughter to be part of the solution, not a part of the problem.

- Teach your daughter to write her older self a love letter from her younger self with all that she hopes she will be mentally, spiritually, and emotionally. Demand at least one commitment from her that she must pinky swear to keep to her younger self. Tell her older self about her career aspirations, what she wants in a spouse, and how to know she is a good friend to others *and* to herself. Tell her older self that her dad is still silly and serious in only the way he can be and that she is still his joy, his laugh, his tears, his twinkle, his daughter.

- Teach her how to tell whether a guy is good or not by getting him in front of dogs and children as soon as possible and watching how he treats the waiters and waitresses.

- Teach her that when she gives her body to a man, she is leading with her heart, but he is likely leading with only his body. Go slow, be careful, be sure.

- Teach her that she is amazing, she is beautiful, she is precious, she is special, and she deserves only the best.

- Teach her to never settle.

"My Dad Taught Me ..."
Tips shared by daughters

- My dad taught me what he called "opportunity thinking." In every situation, ask yourself, "What's the opportunity?" It taught me to always think forward and search for how I could make the most out of every situation. I owe my business brain to him!

- My dad taught me if you don't create debt, you won't have any.

- My dad taught me if you lend something to somebody, just give it to them instead. If you never get it back, there are no hard feelings.

- My dad taught me to work through your crises. If you don't, you will create a lot more of them.

- My dad taught me your reputation is everything, so don't mess it up.

- My dad taught me to put a smile on your face, and people won't notice what you're wearing.

- My dad taught me to work hard, and do your best.

- My dad taught me basic car maintenance, like how to check and fill the oil and put air into my tires, which has helped me on many occasions when nobody else was around.

- When driving, my dad taught me to not hit the brakes when going through a curve on the highway. Instead, maintain your speed and steer. That lesson applies to many areas of life as well.

- My dad taught me that relationships can thrive over long distances and that having divorced parents was not a big deal. He called my brother and me every day, even though he and my mom divorced when I was two and only saw us every other weekend after my mom moved us 350 miles away.

- My dad taught me to always think positively, which pretty much sums up my life.

- My dad taught me to never get addicted to anything, words I've carried with me for obvious reasons.

- My dad taught me to step out of my comfort zone. He knew that once I pushed past my fears to do something I would be glad I did. I always had faith that I'd be okay because this big, strong man, my daddy, said so.

- My dad taught me to be proud of my handwriting, always telling me how clear and beautiful it was.

- My dad taught me to always treat others as I want to be treated.

- My dad taught me that love is the greatest gift.

- My dad taught me that if I don't know who I really am, I will fall for anything.

- My dad taught me to always let a man tell you what he will do, but then watch his actions before you believe him. A man's words and actions should always align.

- My dad taught me the more I respect myself, the more that men will respect me.

- My dad taught me confidence by always respecting and complimenting my mom and all the women around me.

- My dad taught me why sports are so important to me by teaching me how to play when I was young.

- My dad taught me to be kind to people on your way up because they will be the same ones you meet on your way down.

- My dad taught me what to expect from boys by taking me on my first date. (He took my daughter on her first date too). He opened the doors, we had a great conversation, and we ate at a real restaurant. (No fast food.) At the end of the evening, he kissed me on the cheek at the front door and left me to go inside by myself. (He went around to the back of the house to go inside. It was precious.) Once inside, he told me that anyone I go out with should have the same amount of respect for me as he did or they weren't worth being with. It was a memory and a lesson I will cherish forever.

- My dad taught me how important it is to be kind by giving one of our neighbor kids a bicycle for Christmas that he really wanted but wasn't going to get from his family. I will never forget that boy's face when he walked into the living room and we were there with his bike. To me, being kind is the most important quality a person can possess.

- My dad taught me table manners—keep your plate clean, chew your food with your mouth closed, and discard all waste into the trash.

- My dad taught me to always have fun with the mundane. I can always make an undesirable task funny.

- My dad taught me strategic thinking through chess and other creative learning games. He taught me how to see the mysteries and intangibles of life by showing me the beauty in learning.

- My dad taught me that I was special and unique.

- My dad taught me to be confident in my driving by saying, "Keep driving on the road you are on; most likely you will run into a highway." I've never been afraid of getting lost.

- My dad taught me that respect is earned. It's not something that comes with money, titles, or status in life.

- My dad taught me to make honesty a priority above pleasing others. And when possible, do both.

- My dad taught me to never stop for gas unless I can see the gas station from the road.

- My dad taught me to always think for myself, despite what everyone says or thinks.

- My dad taught me to be present in the moment and give of my time.

- My dad taught me to always have empathy for others.

- My dad taught me to be independent but that asking for help doesn't mean that I'm weak.

- My dad taught me that happiness is the measure of success.

- My dad taught me the importance of honesty by always encouraging me to be open and truthful with him. As I matured, I never felt men were scary, or dangerous, or better than me. I knew I was strong, knowledgeable, and equal.

- My dad taught me how valuable I was because he always walked on the outside of a sidewalk, closest to the curb. He would say, "A man always protects a woman from danger, seen and unseen."

- My dad taught me how to throw a solid punch to defend myself.

- My dad taught me to never second-guess myself about whether I locked a door. He taught me to turn the knob from side to side as I say to myself, "This door is locked."

- My dad taught me that it's nobody else's responsibility to make me happy—that's my job.

- My dad taught me to treat everyone with the same respect, from trash collectors to CEOs.

- My dad taught me to be authentic to myself. If you aren't true to you, you will drive yourself mad and, eventually, the truth will surface anyway.

- My dad taught me to know all the facts if I'm going to argue my point. If I'm not sure of the facts, I don't say anything.

- My dad taught me to never be afraid to take things apart and put them back together.

- My dad taught me how to drive a stick shift and even trusted me to take his car and learn it on my own. Even though I burned the clutch, he didn't make me feel bad; he just repaired it and let me try again until I mastered it.

"I Wish My Father Would Have ..."
Tips shared by daughters

- I wish my father would have taught me how precious a gift a woman's body is.

- I wish my father would have taught me to understand the difference between an indecent touch and a warm hug. And also, to understand what good men really want and look for in a woman.

- I wish my father would have taught me that while all men are not bad, sometimes appearances are deceptive and how to trust myself to know who is safe and who is not.

- I wish my father would have taught me that women can equally contribute in many ways, just like men do.

- I wish my father would have understood enough about himself and his own masculinity to teach me more about understanding men.

- I wish my father would have taught me the importance of personal choice and that I have the whole world to choose from.

- I wish my father would have placed more value on supporting my decision-making journey instead of constantly warning me, disciplining me, shaming me, and scolding me.

- I wish my father was comfortable with me crying and being emotionally hurt.

- I wish my father would have taught me what a healthy marriage looked like and that I was worthy of love and being treated with great kindness and respect.

- I wish my father would have taught me that my worth isn't determined by my success. I wish he would have celebrated me for who I *am* and not what I *do*.

- I wish my father would have hugged and kissed me for no reason at all.

- I wish my father would have asked for help when he needed it.

- I wish my father would have been on time for my piano recitals, plays, and games or at least let me know if he was not going to show up.

- I wish my father would have remembered my birthday every year.

- I wish my father would have loved himself more.

- I wish my father would have had more conversations with me when I was younger and did a lot less yelling.

- I wish my father would have taken me to do things he recommended I should do. For example, when I played soccer, he suggested running sprints. I wish he'd said, "Let's go run sprints."

- I wish my father would have taught me that I am beautiful as I am and that I am worthy of love just simply for being me.

- I wish my father would have taught me how to come up with my own answers instead of always giving me the solutions to my problems. I grew up not feeling like I could make decisions on my own, constantly questioning myself and my intelligence.

Online Resources

PLEASE CONTINUE THIS CONVERSATION at www.CoachSeanSmith.com/girldad for ...
- Free individual coaching
- More resources on fathering, masculinity and men's work
- Watch Sean's one-man play *I Do, Mom*
- Watch Sean's TEDx poem about being a REAL man
- Get your questions answered

Women, book your free coaching session at www.CoachSeanSmith.com/bookmycall

Acknowledgments

Thank you, **Bobby Haas**, for being the best editor possible for this project. You turned it into something much richer and more impactful than I could have ever done on my own.

Thank you, **Polly Letofsky**, for being a wonderful literary midwife through this exquisite journey of creating, publishing, promoting and giving birth to my first book.

Thank you, **Victoria Wolf**, for the incredible front cover which makes my heart skip a beat every time I look at it, and formatting the whole book to be amazing inside and out.

Thank you, **Tony Magee**, for returning my call, the Canada trips, airport sprinting, Nickerson Gardens, all the painfully funny lawnmower convos, and never allowing me to forget my calling.

Thank you, **Jack Canfield**, for showing me what mastery + humility looks like, the countless breakthroughs, the hilarious memories, and being a father figure as I grew up in the industry.

Thank you, **Lisa Nichols**, for the trips around the globe, the new integrity contract, staying solid, and the sheer cacophony of soul-stirring, co-creating, life-changing, gut-busting experiences.

Thank you, **Charcee Starks**, for the immeasurable help, the delirious dance, all the nicknames, getting me addicted to coffee, and making this book as inclusive as possible for all people.

Thank you, **Michelle Moore**, for sending the email, crawling out from under the table, telling me where to go, the unwavering support, and the deep explorations of this delicate topic.

Thank you, **Danita Sajous**, for asking the question in the restaurant, all the Danita-isms, always honoring my mom, and being the ultimate model of the daddy/daughter transformation.

Thank you, **Mom**, for trying one last time after having seven miscarriages, being my biggest online stalker, showing me what unconditional love looks and feels like, your epic monologue scene, and waking me up to share your final three breaths.

Thank you, **Dad**, for being my model of vulnerable masculinity, making all my games, giving me your humor, calling me Seanie, that last bikini joke, teaching me what life is about by jumping off a curb, and living your final eighty days under my roof.

Thank you, **Cindi**, for being such an amazing role model, enduring what you dealt with for ten years between us, making me laugh harder than anyone ever could, keeping my BB gun incident a secret, and being the best sister I could have asked for.

Thank you, **Jeremy**, for first showing me the depth of love I could feel for a nephew, the donut shop question, doing all the tricks with a spoon in your pocket, always bouncing back, the after baseball game jump hugs, and the cherished airport photo.

Thank you, **Cybil**, for that first talk under the stairs, shattering what I thought was possible for love, supporting me through every knuckle-head decision, the midnight walk through Paris, countless soul discussions, superhumanly catching the falling boy, and being my partner parent to two insanely incredible kids.

Thank you, **Ecksley Jeremy**, for all the tickle fights, the pancake flips, the hilarious puns, letting me coach your teams, forgetting the milk story, teaching me the essence of joy, catching your legs in the rails so Mom could make it there, and allowing me to witness the roots of a beautiful man as he grows from boyhood.

Thank you, **McKenna Renae**, for... just, thank you. For poking your head out of Mom's tummy, grabbing a hold of my finger and melting my heart, all the laughs, all the dancing, all the hugs, all the piggy back rides, the water bottle eyes, your wise spirit, your strong mind, your beautiful soul, your pretty smile, being the inspiration for this book, the sacred nose-to-nose picture on the front cover, turning me into a daddy and changing the way I see the world, causing me to touch parts of my soul I didn't know I had, allowing me to understand what the word pride truly means, and, my God, for that precious giggle that takes my breath away every time I hear it. I'm proud of you.

And finally, thank you, **Little Seanie**, for questioning every single thing you saw in this world, the dreams that kept us up at night, the choice to try baseball, your fear of dying, your bigger fear of regretting how we lived, your smarts in school, the extreme determination to make a difference, stargazing for hours and hours, swerving left, somehow getting us out of that slow lane, making me keep that Dec. 17th, 1986 promise to you, waiting until I was ready to release my pain and anger, holding my hand while healing our deepest wounds, sitting me on your lap when you knew I needed you to help me forgive myself in your presence, and co-writing this book. I love you, Seanie. Keep pedaling, keep playing and stay curious, young man.

About the Author

*"BE who you can be. DO what you can do.
And LIVE a good life."*
—Coach Sean Smith

SEAN SMITH IS A personal development coach and lifelong student of human behavior. He has coached, trained, and mentored tens of thousands of people – primarily women – specializing in helping them overcome self-esteem and confidence challenges.

As 2013's "North America's Next Greatest Speaker," Sean is known for his uncanny ability to move the unmovable; to push aside limitations; and to help individuals redefine what success, health, and fulfillment mean to them. After more than fifteen years of motivating audiences all over the world, mentoring business leaders and training coaches, Sean is known for his authenticity and his ability to inspire virtually anyone, from audiences of thousands to intimate groups of professionals.

Sean speaks about and trains on the topics of masculinity, vulnerability, self-esteem, relationships, parenting, leadership, creativity, public speaking, coaching, entrepreneurship and personal development.

Sean lives in Southern California with his wife, Cybil, and the two great joys of their lives, McKenna and Ecksley.

To hire Sean to coach you or your team, you can find him through www.CoachSeanSmith.com